D0779271

WAR ON ERROR

WAR ON ERROR

Real Stories of American Muslims

MELODY MOEZZI

The University of Arkansas Press
Fayetteville
2007

Copyright © 2007 by The University of Arkansas Press

All rights reserved
Manufactured in the United States of America

CLOTH
ISBN-10: 1-55728-854-2
ISBN-13: 978-1-55728-854-7

PAPERBACK
ISBN-10: 1-55728-855-0
ISBN-13: 978-1-55728-855-4

13 12 11 10 09   6 5 4 3 2

Designed by Liz Lester

⊖ The paper used in this publication meets the minimum requirements of the American National Standard for Permanence of Paper for Printed Library Materials Z39.48-1984.

LIBRARY OF CONGRESS CATALOGING-IN-PUBLICATION DATA

Moezzi, Melody, 1979–
    War on error : real stories of American Muslims / Melody Moezzi.
        p.   cm.
    Includes bibliographical references.
    ISBN 978-1-55728-854-7 (cloth : alk. paper)—ISBN 978-1-55728-855-4
(pbk. : alk. paper)
        1. Muslims—United States—Interviews. 2. Muslims—United States—Social
conditions. 3. Islam—United States. 4. Islam—Essence, genius, nature. 5. United
States—Ethnic relations. I. Title.
        E184.M88M64 2007
        305.6'970973—dc22
                                                        2007030137

In the name of God, Most Gracious, Most Merciful.

—QUR'AN, AL FATIHAH (THE OPENING), 1:1

For my beloved sisters,
Romana and Mersedeh.

Contents

Foreword by Professor Abdullahi Ahmed An-Na'im   xi

Acknowledgments   xv

Introduction   xvii

CHAPTER 1	*Melody*	1
CHAPTER 2	*Roxana*	15
CHAPTER 3	*Matthew*	27
CHAPTER 4	*Ameer*	39
CHAPTER 5	*Sarah*	49
CHAPTER 6	*Faisal R.*	59
CHAPTER 7	*Sanida*	69
CHAPTER 8	*Molham*	81
CHAPTER 9	*Willow*	91
CHAPTER 10	*Hafeeza*	107
CHAPTER 11	*Asra*	117
CHAPTER 12	*Faisal A.*	131

Conclusion   151

Glossary   157

Notes   161

Cited, Consulted, and Suggested Readings   165

Foreword

I celebrate this book by Melody Moezzi as a thoughtful and moving effort to come to terms with being an American Muslim from a positive and proactive perspective. This is important to me personally, to my wife and to our children and granddaughter, as we all seek to negotiate and mediate our overlapping identities as American Muslims from Sudan. Melody's gift as a facilitator of free-flowing and intimate conversation is in her ability to bring the warm and spontaneous voices of her subjects to the reader, diminishing her intermediacy and bringing those she interviews into direct conversation and shared reflection with the reader. I also celebrate this book as a global citizen and human rights advocate, because Melody's initiative is about the creative possibilities of diversity and pluralism within and among communities everywhere. The limited purpose of this brief foreword is to provide some background and context for this mediation of identity, from the demographic realities of diversity to an affirmation of the supreme value of pluralism—not only for immigrant and host communities in the United States but also on a global scale.

Throughout history, Muslims have thrived on diversity—ethnic and cultural, as well as religious—which often matured into sustained pluralism. The remarkable historical success of Islam as a world religion can be largely attributed to its ability to adapt to the preexisting religious and cultural experiences of the communities it sought to incorporate over time. Building on the foundational model of the Prophet Muhammad's mission in Western Arabia in the early seventh century, Muslims have always sought to adapt to preexisting social and cultural conditions, with minimal imposition of their own religious or political views and lifestyles. The quality of being Muslim or Islamic has therefore evolved over time as the deeply contextual outcome of constant interaction within and among Islamic families and communities and their neighbors. All elements and processes that determined Islamic identity at any given point in time and place were also the product of dynamic interaction with non-Muslim communities at home and abroad, from sub-Saharan Africa to the Indian subcontinent, from Eastern Europe and Central Asia to Southeast Asia.

Not only have recent Muslim immigrants to Western Europe and North America been formed and transformed by that dynamic mediation of multiple and overlapping identities in their regions of origin, but they also bring with them that knowledge and skill, which they can pass on to their own children and share with wider communities in their newly adopted homes. But this does not mean that such processes of integration and transformation were ever easy, or free of the risk of hegemony and oppression, within and among Islamic families and communities and in their relationships with others. At one level, Muslims have always had to deal with severe, often violent ethnic and theological differences in their local or regional settings. Like all other human beings, Muslims have had to negotiate complex power relations within prevalent patterns of socioeconomic stratification that were often compounded by religious and political hegemony. Immigrant and minority Muslim communities have further had to cope with similar tensions in their relationships with host communities or dominant cultures.

The dynamic nature of such mediation of multiple and overlapping identities has always been shaped by the attitudes and concerns of other communities and how they perceived and interacted with Muslims. This includes similar processes occurring within and among those other communities, whether indigenous or immigrant. Thus, the "sociology of immigration," including how previous cycles of immigration were transformed and incorporate in the United States, for example, is also relevant to the experiences of more recent Muslim immigrants to this country.

In this light, the experiences of Muslim immigrants to the United States and Canada, for instance, can be seen as variations on the ancient theme of adaptation and renegotiation of overlapping identities in new settings. A clear understanding and positive engagement of these adaptations should balance the wisdom of past experiences elsewhere with the specific requirements of these new settings. It is important to appreciate and respect the perspective and experience of children born and raised in this new social and cultural environment. The experience of being born of Muslim parents and raised in the home of Muslim immigrants must be understood on its own terms, rather than assuming it to be a simple replication of the experience of immigrant parents. An effort to understand the experiences of this younger generation should invite recognition of both the commonalities of the immigrant experience and the particularity of being from a Muslim background, even when children do not consciously identify as Muslims.

I have so far deliberately avoided any reference to the post-9-11 environment in the United States, because that should not be taken as the defining framework for this book, despite the serious implications of that tragedy. As an American Muslim who has had to deal with that event and its aftermath throughout the world, I do not believe it appropriate or productive to present this book as a defense of Islam and Muslims. The atrocities of 9-11 are the responsibility of the perpetrators of those crimes against humanity, for which Islam and Muslims at large cannot and should not be held accountable. American Muslims must indeed be concerned about such traumatic events and their consequences, and their responses will no doubt challenge the perpetrators' attempts to justify or rationalize their inhumanity in Islamic terms. But this should not be confused with some assumed or alleged "guilt by association," whereby Islam and Muslims are somehow deemed to share in the responsibility of the perpetrators for those crimes. This cannot be true for Islam and Muslims in the same way that past or current atrocities are not the responsibility of Christians or Hindus, Germans or Irish, simply because they share some religious, ethnic, or cultural affiliation with the perpetrators of such crimes.

The experiences of American Muslims defy simplistic generalizations or categorization. Being Muslim is necessarily a matter of personal experience and individual responsibility that cannot be abdicated. It is therefore appropriate neither to reduce being an American Muslim to a narrow and negative stereotype nor to attribute the actions of Muslims to Islam as such. Islam, or any religion, is not an entity that can act. It is always people who act or fail to act. All people are themselves responsible for their own actions and omissions, and that responsibility cannot be transferred to the community of believers. Given the fact that there has always been so much diversity in views and interpretations among Muslims, it is misleading to take one view as definitive or representative of Islam itself. Melody is therefore right to acknowledge that her subjects herein speak for themselves as Muslim Americans, and not for the whole of the Islamic tradition or for all Muslims. Such an acknowledgment can be liberating, because it provides for plurality and diversity within religious communities, but it can also be problematic when believers abuse their autonomy and freedom of choice. In the final analysis, the message

Melody so effectively communicates through the narratives of her subjects is that there are countless ways to understand and practice Islam. By accepting this great variability, Muslims and non-Muslims can both learn a great deal from one another and achieve greater levels of mutual understanding and appreciation of each other's traditions.

Abdullahi Ahmed An-Na'im, Ph.D.
Charles Howard Candler Professor of Law
Emory University School of Law

November 5, 2006

Acknowledgments

Most of all, I thank all of the brave individuals who appear in the chapters of this book for entrusting me to tell their stories. To Matthew in particular, there's too much; I'd have to be a poet or a romantic to thank you right, and you know I'm neither.

To my parents, thank you for your love, patience, and honesty.

✦✦✦ ✦✦✦

To Larry Malley, for not asking me to go out and find a terrorist to interview, for getting it from the very beginning, and for allowing me more artistic freedom than I knew what to do with.

To Abduh An-Na'im for guiding, educating, and mentoring me—and, of course, for writing the foreword. I also owe a special thanks to Christina M. Girgis and Carol Sickman-Garner for their editorial acumen, as well as to Salman Elmi for his social acumen.

Many thanks to the following individuals for providing shining counterexamples of the idea that being successful in publishing requires brutal insensitivity: Novin Doostdar, Danielle Durkin, Lilly Ghahremani, Lindsay Jones, Geraldine Kennedy, Nancy Love, Anna Lui, Elaine Maisner, Amanda Moon, Joseph Parsons, Charlie Perdue, Betsy Phillips, Cynthia Read, Malcolm Reed, Sophia Seidner, and Carole Stuart.

Each of the following individuals helped to make this book a reality, and I am deeply grateful to them: Nobar Elmi, Sanida Halebic, Roxana Jafarian, and Rushmi Mehan; as well as Daayiee Abdullah, Sarah AbuNama-Elgadi, Faisal Alam, Joran Jamal Al' Belar, Alita Anderson, Sanam Behi, Sherwin Danai, Bob Doto, Sandi DuBowski, Sahar Durali, Ilham Elkoustaf, Ameer Kim El-Mallawany, Roja Fazaeli, Dan Greening, Tiffany Hodge, Willie Knight, Tom and Jean Lenard, Chris Lenard, Miriam Majd, Mario Mathis, Emily Monroy, Ayla Nejad, Asra Nomani, Emile Pinera, Lindsay Pratt, Sandra Pullman, Hafeeza Rashed, Soraya Rofagha, Avi Salzman, Hootan Shahidi, Sara Shandler, Parvez Sharma, Fariba Shoarinejad, Edgar Pierre Simard, Laurel Snyder, Howard Spiro, Dara Tabesh, Shireen Tawil, Siva Vaidhyanathan, Natalie Ware, and G. Willow Wilson.

Finally, I thank two teachers who changed the direction of my life: Barry Peters and Larry Schenk from Centerville High School. Were it not for either one of you, I wouldn't be a writer or an activist today. I will never be able to thank you enough for all that you have taught me, for purchasing my first subscription to *Harper's*, or for sacrificing your own time to supervise the Amnesty International group that I started as my first step into the world of social activism. You have both changed my life, and I pray that one day I may be able to have a small fraction of the effect on someone else that you had on me.

Introduction

I decided to write this book to tell the stories of my fellow American Muslims, stories I felt weren't being told. I wanted to affirm the experiences of Muslim Americans as *American* experiences, as grounded in the American dream and the American ethic as any others. The stories here are but a few of many, yet they suffice to verify that the phrase "Muslim American" is neither an oxymoron nor a predicament of circumstance. These are American stories, and until we begin to see and hear them as such, we will never fully understand or appreciate ourselves as Americans.*

First, let me make it absolutely clear that I am no Islamic scholar and that this book is not some clean and organized academic exercise. I have found no way to neatly package the realities of living as a Muslim American today—they are too diverse, complex, and multifaceted to confine to even a hundred books, let alone one. As a Muslim American woman who does not particularly enjoy how her faith is being globally misrepresented and misunderstood, however, I cannot just let all of this misinformation slide because the task of clarification is just too great or complicated. Though I may not be an imam or an Islamic scholar, I am a thinking, feeling, educated, and stubborn Muslim Iranian American woman, and I've done my research. Being less impressed with titles and tidiness than with truth, moreover, I'm finally ready to compile the unruly results. I have written this book in a very personal attempt to foster a kind of greater understanding and respect for Islam and Muslims, which I believe can only be achieved through recognizing (amid all of our messy differences, contradictions, and inconsistencies) one shared humanity.

Though much has been written and said about "Islamic fundamentalism" and so-called political Islam post-9-11, the stories of the millions of individual

---

*The terms *American* and *America* are inherently broad and ambiguous, as they include all of North, Central, and South America. In the context of this book, however, for the sake of brevity and with no intended disrespect to the extensive nature of the Americas, I use such terms to refer to the United States, and not to the Americas as an entirety, unless otherwise noted.

Muslims, and in particular Muslim Americans, with no understanding of or relation to this infamous version of "Islam" have received much less attention.* Understandably to an extent, those who commit horrific acts of violence and destruction, whether in downtown Manhattan, Oklahoma City, Columbine, or Waco, tend to receive much more airtime than those who go about their daily lives trying to do good.

There's no debate that violence and sensationalism sell. Nevertheless, having interacted with a much more mundane and less violent crowd—growing up in Dayton, Ohio; going to college in Middletown, Connecticut; waiting tables on Manhattan's Upper West Side; and attending graduate school in Atlanta, Georgia—I am certain that the everyday stories of even just those individuals whom I have happened to meet and befriend throughout my short life in this country are much more intriguing, insightful, and edifying than those of Muhammad Atta, Timothy McVeigh, or Ted Kaczynski. I wrote this book because I have faith that Americans can and want to see past the sensationalism to something real.

Islam holds that all those who surrender to God (including non-Muslims, and Jews and Christians in particular) shall "have their reward with their Lord; on them shall be no fear, nor shall they grieve" (2:62). While some Muslims may claim that only Muslims, or for that matter even only Sunni or Shi'ite Muslims, can ever hope to attain Paradise or Heaven or spiritual deliverance, the Qur'an clearly states otherwise. Such contradictions in practice have misled and misinformed both Muslims and non-Muslims. Thus, before the Muslim community can expect to be understood and accepted by the "Western world," individual Muslims must first understand and accept Islam, not as it is fed to them by religious and political leaders (who often have their own misguided views and agendas) but as they find it themselves within the Qur'an.†

The trend in much of today's Western media, moreover, to demonize Islam and the so-called Islamic world is not nearly as devastating to Islam or the

---

*All references to September 11 or 9-11 refer to September 11, 2001.

† Broad labels such as "the Western world," "the West," "the East," "the Islamic world," "the Muslim world," and so on, are all potentially dangerous, as they often falsely imply some sort of clear distinction between the East and the West or the Islamic world and the Western world. While, indeed, no clear and absolute distinction exists, I use such references sparingly and with no intended misdirection. My intention is simply to broadly distinguish between European-influenced cultures (where Christianity is the predominant faith) and Asian- or African-influenced cultures (where Islam is the predominant faith).

"Islamic world" as it is and has the potential of being to America and the American national identity. As no one race, religion, or ethnicity alone defines "Americanness," in the same way that they might in more ethnically and/or religiously homogenous countries such as Pakistan, Japan, Iran, or Iceland, for example, demonizing or excluding any one race, religion, or ethnicity has a potentially far more devastating impact on U.S. national identity and unity than it ever could in a more culturally homogenous country. By demonizing "the other," we demonize ourselves as Americans, for "the other" is more American than anyone else. Thus, the greatest threat to our country today comes not from the outside but rather from within, and I hope that these stories help transform this looming threat, and the fear that accompanies it, into security, self-respect, and understanding among Muslims and non-Muslims alike.

〃〃 ↘↘↘

Statistics have never much interested me, as they are highly prone to manipulation. Nevertheless, people seem to be fascinated by them and the false sense of security that they provide, so to avoid disappointment, here goes: The least contested statistics rank Islam as the second-largest religion in the world, with nearly 1.3 billion adherents (around 20 percent of the world's population—with roughly 69 percent in Asia, 27 percent in Africa, and less than 4 percent in other parts of the world, including, but certainly not limited to, parts of the Middle East).[1] Islam is also often identified as the world's fastest-growing religion.[2] Statistics documenting the number of Muslims in the United States vary from 2 to 6 million.[3] Soon after 9–11, a great deal of attention was given to claims that previous estimates of Muslim Americans had been inflated.[4] Since then, however, these low estimates and contentions regarding inflated figures have largely and unsurprisingly dissipated. The 2007 *World Almanac*, citing the World Christian Database, estimated a Muslim American population of 4,657,005 individuals.[5]

Perhaps the most surprising statistics for many Americans are those indicating that only roughly 12 percent of Muslims around the world are in fact Arab, especially given much of the American media's and even academia's tendency to treat Islam as an exclusively Arab phenomenon.[6] Perhaps this is because Mecca is located in what is now Saudi Arabia or because the Qur'an was revealed in Arabic, but whatever the source of this misconception, it is indeed a prominent one. As a result, many of the social and cultural customs within the Arab world have been misunderstood and mistaken for Muslim ones, and vice versa. Islam does not claim one race, nationality, or ethnicity, and thus, it cannot be effectively understood through regional circumstance. The personal stories herein demonstrate a wide array of distinct regional experiences, coinciding with equally distinct Muslim experiences, and my hope is that these individual lives and experiences together reveal that the need to separate and label is antithetical to the very essence of Islam. If anything, the stories that follow identify the one unifying principal condition of Islam as that of submission to One Compassionate, Omniscient, Merciful, and Benevolent Creator, Who is inherently too great to fit into one humanly delineated category of race, nationality, or even religion.

The "selection process" I employed in choosing the individuals included in this book was far from scientific. There was no random sampling or statistical analysis involved. Rather, I chose these individuals according to the same bases upon which I wrote this book: friendship, honesty, and diversity. It became clear very early on that I was not going to be able to easily construct and fill *categories* of Muslim Americans. If I was going to be at all successful in helping to create a meaningful understanding of Islam and what it means to be a Muslim American, I wasn't going to do it with a statistical sampling—thank God! Besides the fact that I am absolutely lousy at statistics and find them dull, lifeless, and easily manipulated, there was also my deep-seated mistrust of the accuracy of statistics, as applied to *human beings* in particular. I knew that I would have to get seriously personal in writing this book, and it turns out, people tend not to open up to surveys and Scantrons.

As a result, I began by talking with and interviewing friends and friends of friends. I started my search for subjects with those closest to me and then moved out to others with whom I was less familiar, generally recommended by ever-extending strings of friends of friends of friends of friends. I interviewed many people whose stories do not appear herein, simply because I found some stories and individuals more candid and compelling than others. Most significantly, though, I chose these particular stories because I believe that, as different as they all are, they share one very important commonality: honesty. It's not easy to get people to speak honestly about issues of faith to begin with, but to get Muslim Americans to talk about their *personal* practice and understanding of Islam is even more difficult at the moment because of an increased general American hostility to the faith, no matter how irrational, since September 11, 2001.

Clearly, there was a reason I was moved to write this book *after* 9–11: that day prompted a sharp turn in much American public opinion with respect to Islam (from general ignorance and apathy to general ignorance, fear, and hatred). I began writing this book shortly after 9-11, and my timing in doing so was no coincidence: I could no longer justify remaining silent in the face of this ignorance, as once it had been compounded with such strong fear and hatred, that ignorance became much more threatening to me and my fellow Muslim Americans. My "subjects" were well aware of my reasons for tackling this topic at this particular point in American history, and those whose stories appear in the following pages showed a courage unmatched by most—the courage to be honest about their beliefs, their feelings, their thoughts, their pasts, their insecurities, their wants, their fears, and most importantly, their hopes.

Each one of these individuals, moreover, has had a highly unique and intensely personal impact on me, and I feel sincerely blessed by their entry into my life. We are all, especially in America, living in a chaotic context, surrounded by interesting and amazing people. But it's so much easier to ignore the context, to go straight to the *CliffsNotes*, to submit to literalism, and to stick to ourselves and our own "kind," whatever that may be. Easier, however, is rarely more accurate, more insightful, or more fun than its infinite alternatives. Despite the vast differences among the individuals profiled here, not a single one of them can be neatly and easily packaged or classified. Thus, I would be misguided and mistaken to pretend that I could ever *fully* understand any one of them. Still, I believe that it is entirely possible to wholly respect, appreciate, and even love individuals without having to completely understand them. This is, in fact, the essence of compassion, which I have always found to be much more practical and powerful than any illusion of some imaginary, generic, one-size-fits-all type of so-called understanding.

Thus, if I am going to be honest with myself, my readers, and my "subjects," the most that I can assert (without inviting and immediately drowning in a rush of inductive and deductive fallacies) is that it's not easy to be a Muslim American today. There are indeed far easier things to be, but nothing is harder than living a lie. If we, as Muslim Americans of all different varieties, continue being unapologetically our radically different selves, then we are contributing to further understanding every time we meet and interact with other people—and it is this kind of very simple understanding, based on human experience and interaction, that will eventually, little by little, change feelings, attitudes, and opinions. It becomes harder to hate a religion the more good folk you encounter who subscribe to that religion. It's a very simple concept, but I think it deserves some serious consideration.

Muslims vary in their lives and their experiences at least as much as the reader will find that Faisal R. and Faisal A. do. The fact that they share the same name says very little, if anything, about who they are. To know that takes time. To find out who they truly are, you have to sit down with them, really get to know them one-on-one, preferably over food and/or beverage, in a relatively safe and calm environment. People don't get to do that so often anymore. With e-mail and instant messages and text messages and God-knows-what-else, human contact has seriously diminished over the past twenty years, and that is perhaps the most dangerous thing about turning us all into tech-savvy consumers, with our eyes glued to CNN as we walk in place on an indoor treadmill going nowhere, avoiding eye contact with any other three-dimensional human in the vicinity. The moment technology, whether television or cell phones or the Internet, becomes an excuse not to *see* or *touch* or *talk* to someone, it ceases to be the great boon that it's made out to be.

That moment allows for the depersonalization of experience, and it increases the potential for errors in understanding and communication. Certain things cannot be sent over e-mail: a smirk, a shrug, a laugh, a furrowed brow, a nudge, a hug. These are things to be cherished and maintained, for without them, crude discrimination and stereotyping become possible, if not inevitable. There is no emoticon for genuine compassion, just as there is no substitute for actual human contact.

Video games and virtual reality, for example, are inherently inhuman. To boot, they breed obesity, violence, indolence, and stupidity, and so much of my generation is so unbelievably enamored with this garbage. There is something about hearing an actual human voice or holding an actual human hand or looking an actual human being in the eye that cannot be re-created in even the most advanced laboratory. At some point, even the written word fails us. This isn't easy for me to say, seeing as how I am in the business of the written word, but as glorious as it can be, it still falls short when it comes to reaching the deepest levels of human consideration and ultimately compassion.

No matter how clever I might be with words, for example, there is no way I can fully convey the enormous pressure of Roxana's petite arms nearly breaking your ribs in one of her standard hugs, or the look of supreme satisfaction on Matthew's face after he's eaten a good meal and settled in with our purring cat on his lap and a good book in his hands, or the quiet confidence in Ameer's hip and easygoing gait, or the sheer physical and mystical formidability of Sarah's signature afro, or the astonishing quickness with which Faisal R. can jump from aloof philosopher to entertaining jokester to model citizen. Nor can words ever fully capture the way that Sanida speaks with her entire body at outrageously loud volume (even louder when she's laughing) and completely without end if you let her, or the perfect firmness in Molham's typical handshake, or the steady and assured poise in Willow's ethereal voice, or the inimitable evil grin that overcomes Hafeeza's face when she knows she's crossed some obvious social or physical boundary or is about to, or the sweet smell of youth and newness that permeates everything in Asra's home and on her person, or the warmth that appears to be so constantly exuding from Faisal A. Still, as words are all I have, I can't help but try.

ONE

Melody

It is not righteousness
That ye turn your faces
Towards East or West;
But it is righteousness—
To believe in God
And the Last Day,
And the Angels,
And the Book,
And the Messengers;
To spend of your substance,
Out of love for Him,
For your kin,
For orphans,
For the needy,
For the wayfarer,
For those who ask,
And for the ransom of slaves;
To be steadfast in prayer,
And practice regular charity,
To fulfill the contracts
Which ye have made;
And to be firm and patient,
In pain (or suffering)
And adversity,
And throughout
All periods of panic.
Such are the people
Of truth, the God-fearing.

—QUR'AN, AL BAQARAH (THE COW), 2:177

I've had enough of someone else's propaganda.
I'm for truth, no matter who tells it.
I'm for justice, no matter who it is for or against.
I'm a human being first and foremost, and as such,
I'm for whoever and whatever benefits humanity as a whole.

—MALCOLM X, THE AUTOBIOGRAPHY OF MALCOLM X

My parents, especially my father, have always cautioned me against religion in general, and for the most part, they have been right in doing so. They never fully endorsed the practice of one religion to the exclusion of any others in raising either my sister or myself. This is perhaps why I was so adamant in my initial refusal to write this chapter. It took a great deal of goading from my agent at the time to do it, and even then, I must admit that I began writing reluctantly. But ultimately, I did write it, not because my agent wanted me to but because I thought it was only fair to subject myself to the same scrutiny to which I had subjected all of the other individuals whose stories I had been entrusted to tell in the pages of this book. I couldn't very well bring myself to tell the stories of others from my own admittedly subjective standpoint if I hadn't first laid out where that subjectivity was coming from.

The last time I remember going to a mosque with my family, I must have been seven or eight years old. We had gone to this mosque in downtown Dayton every couple of weeks since I could remember, and I liked it mostly because they always had doughnuts, which we never had at home, and because the kids were always just playing hide-and-seek when they weren't eating doughnuts. On that last visit, we were greeted by police. The mosque had been vandalized by some neo-Nazi kids who apparently thought it was a synagogue. It was covered in swastikas, and the windows were all broken. We stopped going after that because my dad said it wasn't safe, and eventually, my sister and I started going to piano lessons instead, which I hated because I was always being upstaged at recitals by this Korean prodigy half my age and, to top it off, there were never any doughnuts.

If anything, the religion of our household was education, and focusing on one tradition of any variety—religious, cultural, or otherwise—would only limit our education. My parents had no problem sending us to a Catholic school when it was the best school in our district, and they had no problem sending me to live with nuns in Spain to study alone at the University of Madrid when I was only sixteen because my Spanish teacher assured them that it would be a priceless educational experience. My dad used to make me look up and write down every new word I heard or read in the English language in a steno pad, and he would test me on them weekly. He refused to let me get away with having less than perfect English just because he did.

More than anything else, though, he refused to let me have a chip on my shoulder just because I was the child of immigrants, or looked different from most other kids growing up in Dayton, or spoke a different language, or didn't worship Christ. There was an absolute prohibition on bitching about that kind of thing in the Moezzi household. I remember going to a slumber party in the eighth grade and having a couple of girls corner me as I was trying to go to sleep. They insisted that I accept Jesus Christ as the Son of God before I fell asleep, and they assured me that if I didn't, there was no doubt that I was going to hell. They told me that they wanted to be able to hang out with me in heaven because I was fun and that I had to accept the Savior before I went to sleep that night or we couldn't hang out later. I kept telling them that I thought Jesus was cool and all, and that I thought that he was a Prophet, but that I didn't think God was up for conceiving children. After what seemed like hours, they finally lost hope and left me alone, but not before reminding me that I was definitely going to hell now. When I told my dad about this, he laughed and told me I should have just said, "Yeah, sure, whatever you say," and gone to sleep. When I told him I didn't want them to have the satisfaction, he told me that if I cared so much about God, I wouldn't care what they said or thought.

That same year, when a deathly pale, chubby, redheaded, freckled girl told me that she could no longer be my friend because her mom said that she should have more Christian friends, I was so shocked that I again told my dad, somehow forgetting that whining about such things was strictly forbidden. He told me that he was happy because he could barely stand looking at her, she was so ugly, and that he wished she had said so earlier, before she threw up in our basement at my thirteenth birthday party.

✧✧✧ ✧✧✧

Both my parents witnessed and lived through Iran's Islamic Revolution—partly in Iran and partly from the United States. I was born in the spring of 1979, at the height of this revolution, not in Iran like my parents but in the middle of America. Having experienced the revolution and its aftermath, my parents have always been understandably averse to anything overtly religious. They have always strongly advised me never to be the one to bring up the topic of religion, particularly Islam, in conversation or writing—especially with or intended for American audiences: "They'll think you're a fanatic; they'll stop taking you seriously; they don't know any better; it just doesn't *look* good." They're right. It doesn't *look* good, in most of the so-called Western world, to say that you are Muslim. But as I age, I am growing less and less concerned with appearances. I am not a terrorist; I do not think women are scum; I do not hate Jews; and I am neither Arab, nor do I speak Arabic.

I don't mean to make presumptions about my reader here. I say all of this as a response to stereotypes with which I have been presented consistently throughout my life. People seem to always want to know what I think about these things when they find out that I am Muslim. Instead of asking about Islam, they ask me what I think of the Israeli-Palestinian debacle or feminist ideals or terrorism. These issues, which are inherently political and/or criminal in nature, have much to do with power and manipulation, but nothing to do with faith. Still, I admit that, even though I don't want it to, at least one such association manages to cross my *own* mind when a stranger tells me that she or he is Muslim.

This type of disgusting Pavlovian response is, to me, the worst form of cultural oppression, and it is my sincere belief that such oppression can only be combated through education—not necessarily through academia, but through learning, compassion, and understanding. This belief, along with a personal attraction to truth and any journey that might lead to it, most fully explains my motivation in writing this book. Nevertheless, it took a series of unexpected personal experiences, followed by the appalling events of 9-11 and the worldwide response to them, before I could manage to write a single word.

※※ ※※

Several years before 9-11, I was faced with a personal awakening disguised, as many are, in the form of adversity. After nearly twenty years of good health and good fortune, I got sick. The saga began directly after my senior year of high school. My graduation party was shared with several other graduates, all members of our large Dayton Iranian community of friends, who had been my second family since childhood. It was in the ballroom of a Holiday Inn near the Dayton Mall. I remember doing a lot of dancing and consuming an inhuman amount of junk food—brownies, Doritos, cookies, cake—all courtesy of the hotel caterers, who wouldn't allow us to bring our own food. If Iranians know how to do anything, they know how to throw parties, and to our parents' credit, this party (apart from the catering) was no exception.

I wore a bright yellow, knee-length flowing chiffon dress with spaghetti straps. When I look at the pictures now, I cringe. I look like a banana with a little brown head and long flailing limbs to match. Still, all of our friends and family kept telling me how beautiful I looked and how proud they were of my personal and academic accomplishments. My dad, to this day, still says that I was the victim of the evil eye, and that had he burned *esfand* (a heavy, strong-smelling incense that, according to Persian superstition, is supposed to ward off the evil eye) over my head that night, this all probably would have never happened. I don't think he really believes it though.

That night, after opening more gifts than I had ever received in my life, I started having slight stomach pains. They were still there the next day, and by the next night I was in excruciating pain. My parents kept insisting that it was just gas, but I forced them to take me to the emergency room anyway. They were so convinced of the triviality of my condition, though, that they made a pit stop at the Elmis' house en route to the hospital. The Elmis were going to Iran the next day, and my dad insisted that if we didn't drop off the standard shipment of medicines for them to bring along, a bunch of our family members in Iran, short on necessary medications, would be forced to suffer severe mental and physical hardships—all thanks to me and my unrelenting gas.

The Elmis, while not blood relations, have been my second family since I can remember, and while I would generally be excited to see them, I was far from thrilled to be delaying immediate medical attention. Still, being a sucker for guilt trips and genuinely wanting to avoid responsibility for the ill health of anyone in Iran, I grudgingly agreed to the short visit and tried to tolerate the delay by staying in the car, waiting in the backseat with my knees pressed tightly against my chest, and rocking back and forth to distract myself from the pain. I remember that Dr. Elmi—the dad, an orthopedic surgeon, my godfather (who would oversee the ceremony of my marriage some five years later), and Amoo Ali to me (*amoo* meaning "paternal uncle" in Farsi)—came out of the house to offer me some Tylenol. I tried to be polite in refusing it, but I'm sure I came off as a total brat, which at that point in my life was far from an anomaly. I was sure that nothing short of some seriously heavy narcotics could control this pain, and as it turned out, despite my inexperience, I was right.

I was sobbing uncontrollably by the time we got to hospital, and I was rushed into an examination room. After a few lab tests, it became clear that I was having an attack of acute pancreatitis, a sudden inflammation of the pancreas that most commonly affects overweight, middle-aged alcoholic men and people with gallstones—none of which came close to describing me. Everyone was convinced I had been doing some heavy postgraduation celebratory drinking, but after I assured them that I didn't drink at all and that I had not recently been bitten by a snake or a scorpion (apparently another likely cause), the doctors finally ordered a CT scan.

The results suggested the presence of a pseudocyst in the middle of my pancreas, and that night, I nearly died of shock resulting from the pancreatitis. That same night, the doctors arranged to send me via helicopter to a hospital in Indiana for specialized care. I vaguely remember receiving my last rites from a priest before leaving the hospital and being too drugged up to explain to him that I wasn't Christian and too desperate at that point to reject *anyone's* prayers on my behalf.

Not a fan of flying, I asked if we could just drive instead, and while the doctors weren't encouraging, my parents gave in and drove me the one hundred miles to Indianapolis, hanging my IV on the coat hook in the backseat. I made it through the night and was treated for a week in Indianapolis—the treatment consisting mainly of starvation. After that, I started becoming familiar with hospitals around the country. For the next two years, as modern medicine tried to fix me, I was placed on a restrictive diet and underwent several endoscopic procedures in an effort to avoid surgery, all to no avail.

On the morning of April 1, 1999, I was admitted to Chicago's Rush Presbyterian Hospital to undergo a risky invasive operation the name of which I can't pronounce to this day. During the week after the surgery, my family and I were presented with a series of details about my condition: first, I had a tumor, not a cyst; second, this tumor was malignant, and the cancer had spread to outlying tissues; third, I had roughly a year left to live; and finally, two days later, that some dye hadn't been picked up on a few slides, and I had correspondingly been misdiagnosed: the tumor was in fact benign. I was going to live.

〳〳〳 〵〵〵

All of this happened while I was an undergraduate at Wesleyan, a freethinking, picturesque liberal arts university in the central Connecticut valley. At the time, I was busy burying my head in the writings of old dead white men, mostly philosophers. I read all of the works assigned assiduously, hoping to reach some great spiritual awakening through reason. Getting sick, however, inspired the collapse of most of my rational faculties for a good while. After being admitted to the ER on several occasions for eating foods that my pathetically deficient pancreatic enzymes were failing to digest—a chocolate chip muffin, overly oiled pasta, anything fried—I made the unilateral decision to stop eating all together.

I had always been thin, and I had never taken any active notice of the food that I put into my mouth or the power that action entailed until I was forced to monitor it, literally to save my life. Out of frustration and despair, I took things to an extreme. As a result, I spent half of my college career with a raging eating disorder and the other half in recovery, undergoing intensive outpatient treatment in the form of psychotherapy, which, by the grace of God, worked.

While I had endured extreme physical pain because of my pancreatic condition, it never came close to matching the pain I inflicted on myself. I have no doubt that I lost my mind for almost two years there, and *that*, not a tumor, was what led me to start contemplating the most selfish of all human acts. I fantasized about suicide incessantly for a period, and by refusing to ingest food, I was well on my way. Every day there was less and less of me, and somehow I found this comforting. My only other comfort was in books, but after a point, all of the philosophers started to sound the same, and I began to question their intentions in writing anything at all.

It was upon reaching this state of desperation that I took an unknowing step toward God, and before I knew it, He had taken a thousand toward me. Having never read the central text underlying the religion to which I had always claimed to subscribe, I decided, out of boredom and frustration with the great rational philosophers, to read the Qur'an. I intended to read it as a break, and began as a literary critic approaching a new genre, but I finished feeling like a naive and misinformed child. To my surprise, I had only three or four points of contention upon completing the text, and those were mostly resolved through a little deeper thought and/or reconciling translations from English to Farsi to Arabic. I had expected, at best, to find the kind of insight I'd found in great novels. My expectations, however, were far surpassed. I had unwittingly found a path that looked as if it could work for me, and the fact that this path accepted the viability of other paths and other pilgrims was what most convinced me of our compatibility.

It was then that I chose to retrieve my mind. After having read less than half of the Qur'an, I began to feel a strength and ease previously unknown to me. It was this strength that finally led me to seek help for my eating disorder on my own terms, for as my family and friends had all made countless well-intentioned attempts to help before, I had not yet been ready to do the work. It was a year after starting this treatment for my eating disorder that I finally underwent surgery to remove the growing mass in my viscera. The final and most pleasant part of my recovery took place less than one month after I was released from the hospital, when, against the advice of my surgeon, my parents, and most everyone who cared, I chose to drive cross-country to spend the summer in the most beautiful territory I had ever, or since, beheld.

I got a job folding T-shirts and making fudge and espresso at a resort at the edge of Glacier National Park, near the Canadian border, and I spent every minute I wasn't working in awe. I learned the words of the Prophet Muhammad's daily prayers in Arabic and, most importantly, their meaning. I began to pray through speaking those delightfully melodic words for the first time in my life. I started carrying an extra set of prayer "materials" in my car: a large soft sheet, or chador, to cover my body (so that I could more easily focus on my soul) and a small prayer rug to keep my feet from getting dirty.

I became increasingly dedicated to performing each of the daily prayers, a practice that has always brought me great solace but that has also, since I learned how to do it, admittedly become a fairly constant source of guilt as well, given my lousiness at it. Today, on a good day, I generally do one or two of the formal prayers, but I am a work in progress. Montana will always maintain a spiritual quality for me, not simply because of its breathtaking scenery but because it was the place where I first fully embraced my faith. Neither before nor since my time there has my practice ever been so disciplined.

Amid the mountains, lakes, and receding glaciers of northwestern Montana, without a mosque, a mullah, or even another Muslim to be found, I came to believe fully, not only in the power, presence, and beauty of God but also in the fact that He had a plan for me and that His grace, patience, and mercy refused to let me forget it. Thus began my genuine attempt to pursue the path of Islam.

I was aware of and experienced a general ignorance about Islam among most Americans, but it was a harmless ignorance, in that I ran across only a few people who actually hated me for having this background or belief. The great majority just didn't know what being Muslim meant, and while they may have had some negative associations with the faith, their ignorance usually prevented them from stating or acting on them.

In Montana, I worked with many other young men and women, mostly college students as well, and to my recollection every single one was Christian —a significant minority of them Mormons, with whom I generally formed a unique bond, given that they were my sole companions in sobriety. While most of them took that sobriety to greater lengths than I (I avoided only alcohol, and they often avoided caffeine as well), there was still clearly a connection based on our mutual distaste for mind-altering substances and the inane behaviors that often result from their consumption. Not a single one of the Mormons I met, moreover, ever held it against me that I worked as a barista at the resort's espresso bar, nor did a single one of them ever actively try to convert me. They knew what it was like to be in the minority, and I think that shared reality helped them steer clear of any missionary work with me as the object.

I remember some of my friends "warning" me about the Mormons, so that I would be prepared for their assumed future attempts to convert me. If anything, however, the Mormons I met in Montana turned out to be my staunchest supporters and defenders. Strange things happen when you're stuck in the middle of nowhere with a bunch of imported college students, there only for the summer. For me, I quite unexpectedly ended up learning a great deal about Mormonism—not by reading the Book of Mormon, which embarrassingly I have yet to pick up, but by meeting and befriending some of its adherents. Likewise, my guess is that my newly befriended Mormon brothers and sisters (none of whom, in all probability, had ever picked up a copy of the Qur'an) got some rather unexpected basic instruction in Islam through our friendships as well.

In a lot of ways, Mormons tend to get a bad rep based on the actions of a few crazy missionaries, just like Muslims tend to get a bad, if not worse, rep based on the actions of a few crazy terrorists. Comparing lunatics aside, the great majority of us are pretty decent people, Muslim and Mormon alike. Turns out that neither is quite that scary after all.

Nevertheless, I was still not only the sole Muslim in residence but the sole non-Christian, brown girl who wasn't a member of the Blackfeet Tribe. There were no Blacks, no Asians, no Arabs, no Hispanics. Just white Americans, Canadians, the Blackfeet, and me.

This brings me to Elizabeth, a girl I worked with at the St. Mary's Lodge and Resort gift shop. Elizabeth was a constant source of amusement for the rest of us, as she was incredibly ignorant in most matters. Nevertheless, she was very sweet and bore no ill will toward anyone. People would come in asking for books on Indian paintbrushes, some of the most popular wildflowers in the park, and she would tell them that we only had normal paintbrushes and that maybe they should drive down to the reservation and ask the Indians about them. She asked me one afternoon, after catching me praying outside, what religion I was. I told her that I was Muslim, and in response, she asked me what denomination of Christianity "Muslim" was. I told her that it was kind of like being Methodist, not being in the mood for long explanations.

✂✂ ⟩⟩⟩

I regret my selfish laziness and arrogance now. Today, the explanations are ten times as long, as the assumptions and perceptions are ten times as misguided. Now, instead of taking a couple of minutes to tell the Elizabeths of the world that Indian paintbrushes are wildflowers and that Islam is a separate religion from Christianity but with similar moral bases, I feel compelled to write an entire book.

Some two years before perhaps the greatest public disservice that has ever been performed for Islam, I began my very private conversion through prayer, study, and thought. Thus, when several murderous, thickheaded zealots crashed civilian airliners into the World Trade Center towers and the Pentagon on September 11, 2001, my first reactions were tears, prayers, and fear. Soon after these subsided, however, I had another familiar response, one that has always accompanied witnessing such mindless, vicious, and surreal acts: "Please, God. Don't let these fools end up claiming Islam." But they did, and I prayed that people would see past the idiocy and sensationalism and realize that they could have claimed anything and it wouldn't matter because they were still murderers of innocent men, women, and children, and I am not aware of any God-loving religion that rewards, encourages, or tolerates such slaughter.

Soon after 9–11, some drunken hick drove his truck into a Hindu temple near my parents' house in Dayton, thinking it was a mosque. A friend's uncle, who is Sikh, was slammed over the head by a two-by-four in a Rochester Home Depot solely because the perpetrator thought his turban alone meant he was Muslim, and therefore deserving. My best friend, Christina, and her family, along with the large Coptic Egyptian community in Dayton, got so much crap from people who thought they were Muslim that they eventually had to schedule an information session to inform everyone that most of the Egyptians in the district were Christian—and on a side note, it's bad to harass Muslims just for being Muslim anyway.

As Sikhs, Hindus, and Christian Arabs were getting mistaken for Muslims, I was waiting tables and living in a tiny apartment with Michael and Wendell, an interracial gay couple, and their five cats, along with their pug, Lilly, whom they had brilliantly trained to use a litter box as well. The apartment, in the middle of a largely Dominican and Puerto Rican neighborhood on the Upper West Side of Manhattan, had one window that overlooked a fallout shelter. As the grief and depression that hovered over New York quickly turned into mis-directed rage, slues of Arab-run businesses were being vandalized and harassed all over the city. Muslim women who had previously worn *hijab* began to refrain from doing so for fear of being attacked, and, overall, hate speech and hate crimes directed toward Muslims and Arabs in particular were seriously on the rise. All the while, I was still being mistaken for a Latina.

Before 9-11, I never felt the need to clarify my origins or faith to those mistaking me for something, anything, else. Everyone in the neighborhood just assumed I was Puerto Rican because I spoke Spanish and because I had brown skin and dark curly hair. I wasn't ashamed of my faith or my heritage. I just didn't see the point in publicizing it unless someone explicitly asked. After 9-11, however, I felt like continuing to "pass" would be wrong.

✗✗✗ ✗✗✗

I was eating an empanada and waiting for my clothes to dry at a local Laundromat not far from my apartment when María, who worked there, and with whom I'd developed a camaraderie, started talking about how happy she was that the two brothers who owned a nearby convenience store had been forced to shut it down. She told me that she should have known better than to have ever bought even a stick of gum from those disgusting Arabs. Then she told me that we were lucky that we had a glorious, civilized, Catholic culture that helped us stick together and succeed. I told her that I liked the brothers and that I used to watch soccer games in the back of the store with them because they had satellite. Then she asked me why the hell I did that, given that all they ever watched were Middle Eastern countries' matches. I had told her twice before that I was Iranian, and it now became clear to me that either she had no idea where Iran was or she wasn't listening to me. "María," I told her, "soy iraní. Soy casi árabe, y soy musulmana."* Tears running down my face, I threw the remainder of my empanada at her and ran home, leaving my laundry to fend for itself.

After talking to Michael and crying some more, I went back that night when I knew María would no longer be working. But she was still there, sitting in a lawn chair on the sidewalk in front of the store watching traffic. I walked straight past her without saying a word, and she followed me in. When I asked her why she was still there, she told me that her shift had ended over an hour ago but that she had stayed to wait for me. At this point, I noticed that someone else's clothes were in my drier and mine were nowhere in sight.

---

*"I am Iranian. I'm almost Arab, and I'm Muslim."

"Damn it! Where the hell are my clothes?" That was the first time I had ever spoken to her in English.

She took my hand and led me to the back of the store, where she had neatly folded all of my clothes and wrapped them in tissue paper. She apologized and told me that she was embarrassed and ashamed. She then thanked me for being honest and for debunking her prejudices through my example. I have no idea where María is today, or what she is doing, or even her last name. Still, I am grateful for her example as well, for she gave me hope in the persistent power of friendship and human interaction, no matter how brief or minimal, to impact our lives and attitudes. Without this hope, I could have never even begun to write this book. I am the product of my experiences, memories, and relations, and so is each one of the individuals around whom the following chapters revolve. These individuals are not characters, they are not case studies, and they are not literary devices. They are all real, and they are all awake and dynamic. As such, each of them has given me an education for which there is no worthy or appropriate degree, and I thank them.

TWO

Roxana

When a (courteous) greeting
Is offered you, meet it
With a greeting still more
Courteous, or (at least)
Of equal courtesy.
God takes careful account
Of all things.

—QUR'AN, AL NISA (THE WOMEN), 4:86

You may try a hundred things,
But love alone will
Release you from yourself.
So never flee from love—
Not even from love in an earthly guise—
For it is a preparation for the supreme Truth.
How will you ever read the Qur'an
Without first learning the alphabet?

—JAMI, FIFTEENTH-CENTURY CLASSICAL
PERSIAN SUFI POET, YUSUF AND ZULAIKHA

Lounging contentedly on the bed in her apartment some thirty-five stories directly above the FDR, Roxana looks at me standing over her and proclaims, "Interview me," as though she were Julia Roberts promoting her next blockbuster. I know this is going to be difficult. I have known Roxana for over eight years now. We met in college at Wesleyan when she was a senior and I was a freshman, and within days, we were inseparable. She was the only other Iranian girl I had heard of at Wesleyan, and she seemed to know everything and everyone there was to know there. We were both loud, opinionated, sarcastic, and naive. We were also both virgins and agreed that men were useful almost solely for opening unyielding jars of pickles and hooking up electronic equipment. Roxana is my dearest girlfriend from college, and that may be part of the reason why she was the first person I chose to interview for this book. That and it gave me a decent excuse to escape the Atlanta summer heat and go shopping and dancing in New York City.

I found it incredibly difficult to get Roxana to sit still and be serious long enough to conduct an interview, but I had a plan. I took her to an Indian restaurant and filled her to the point of near-explosion with samosas and chicken tikka masala. Once I got the impression that fullness had wholly debilitated her, I asked for the check and made my move. By the time we got home, her gorged state made her too weak to mock me or protest, and with a little persuasion, she began to yield.

Roxana is quite possibly the least repressed individual I have ever met. She'll yell when she feels like it, she'll laugh when she feels like it, she'll cry when she feels like it, and she'll dance when she feels like it—the location or circumstance is pure coincidence. Demure is not part of her repertoire. She can be painfully socially inappropriate, but she could never be disingenuous if she tried.

Roxana was twelve when her family left Iran, in the summer of 1988. They left at the end of the eight-year-long Iran-Iraq War, but the end of anything is only apparent in hindsight. Things grew progressively worse toward the end of the war. The Iraqis started bombing Tehran that summer, and that same year, Roxana's paternal grandparents died within seven months of each other. Roxana insists that her dad would never have left Iran and made somewhere else his permanent home as long as his mom was alive, and her death made their departure an imminent possibility. Also, on the night of the first Iraqi missile attack on Tehran, Roxana's maternal aunt died in a car accident. After that, her mom was fainting all the time and had to be put on IV fluids. Just the sound of missiles overhead, or anything akin to it, would send her into a fainting spell.

Thus, Roxana's mom's deteriorating emotional state and her father's loss of his greatest ties to Iran precipitated their flight. Her family began selling various household items—particularly, she remembers a Persian rug. She recalls a man coming to buy the rug and wondering why on earth they were selling it. Of course, her parents wouldn't tell her. They were afraid to tell her. The rug reminded her so much of her uncle Hamid Reza, who was one of the hundreds of thousands of Iranians killed in the war. He was only twenty years old. She can't remember why that rug reminded her so much of him, but it did. After selling it, her father told her that they were going to Japan for health screenings and to obtain their visas.

After less than a year in Japan, they moved to Victoria, British Columbia, staying for only two years before moving to Connecticut, where they continue to live today. Roxana didn't want to leave Iran, and her parents even pushed back their flight a couple of weeks to better prepare her for the transition. Ironically, they left two weeks after the peace treaty between Iran and Iraq was signed. Still, nothing in Iran really got any better after that. The war is a painful open wound in the collective memory of the millions of Iranians who lived through it, and its effects are still apparent today.

I personally remember an incident years after the war had ended. I was in the bathroom of my uncle's house in Tehran when all of the lights went out. I just considered it an untimely blackout. After fiddling around to find the toilet paper and the sink, I came out to find everyone walking in circles, praying frantically. They were all certain that Iraq was bombing again. In reality, the war had ended over five years before, but in the minds and homes of so many Iranians, it was still far from over.

In elementary school, Roxana was often called in from recess on account of Iraqi missiles flying overhead. I'm sure that the American government had no idea how many future Iranian Americans it was helping to create by supporting Iraq in that war, and I'm sure that American was the last thing a good number of those children wanted to become at the time. Still, I'd venture to guess that Roxana was not the only future American on that playground.

Roxana finally became a naturalized U.S. citizen in 1999 at the age of twenty-three, but she was an American long before that. This I can attest to much better than she might ever admit herself. The girl speaks fluent English with no accent, and she talks faster (in both English and Farsi) than anyone I've ever met. She has lived in America for over half of her life, and she admits that when she goes back to Iran to visit her extended family, she realizes how American she truly is. When I ask her what has most shaped her American experience, she responds, "I don't know, dude. MTV. McDonald's. You're not really writing that down, are you?" Of course, I'm writing it down. Is there anything *more* American than music videos, reality television, or Happy Meals? I can't think of much, but that may just be a generational thing. Regardless, there isn't even a word for "sarcasm" in Farsi. Roxana is about as American as, I don't know, MTV or McDonald's. And yes, she is Muslim too.

✦✦✦ ❯❯❯

When I finally interview Roxana, she is a twenty-six-year-old, happy, single Manhattanite racking up debt at NYU's dental school. She aspires to one day open an aesthetic dentistry practice somewhere in Connecticut, close to her parents and close to the city. "All I really want from life," she explains, "is to finish school, get married, have a few kids, be a good mom, be a good Muslim, and help people as much as I can as a dentist—basically, just to live a quiet and happy life."

Roxana admits that thus far she has lived a very quiet and happy life as an American, but she is quick to note one exception in particular. On September 11, 2001, Roxana watched firsthand from several blocks uptown as total strangers managed to take her faith hostage just long enough to kill thousands of innocent civilians and tarnish the name of Islam. Her memories from that day are limited: "Just tons and tons of crying and everyone running around frantically. And smoke and ash everywhere. I was an emotional wreck—I think all of us were."

As she explains her emotions, ranging from panic to sadness to fear to petulance to anger, she points toward downtown through her window, to where the World Trade Center towers once stood, and says, "Just look at that! Just look at that smoky emptiness—that's dead people! It's going to take a hell of a long time for that smoke to clear. Everyone's [cell phone] reception in the city is all fucked up now; people are disoriented because they can't use them as a landmark for south; driving downtown is hell. And besides these minor inconveniences, there's even more misdirected ignorant hatred out there. All these Arab and Pakistani cab drivers are getting so much shit, and my friends who wear *hijab* get these nasty looks and comments walking down the street.

There just hasn't been nearly as much 'uniting' in reality due to this tragedy as all the public-service announcements would make you think. I don't know. It's just annoying that I always have to have some sort of unique opinion about it just because I'm Muslim or Iranian. And honestly, I don't really. It just made me really sad and really pissed, and I think that pretty much sums up the way most of the country felt—no matter what their religion."

Still, everyone has somewhat unique reactions to tragedy and disaster, depending on education, experience, and biology, and in that way Roxana is no different. She remembers overhearing one of the security guards in her building talking that day about how the United States goes to help all these people all over the world and how ungrateful all these underdeveloped, uncivilized countries are. While at the time, she claims, she was too exhausted to comment, she does remember her initial thoughts at hearing this. She thought of her uncle Hamid's death at the hands of the American-backed Iraqi army; she thought of the millions of kids dying in Africa because it's no longer profitable for American drug companies to manufacture the medicines that could easily save their lives; she thought of Bosnia, China, Chechnya; and, like many other Muslim Americans, she thought of the American "relocation" camps where Japanese and Japanese Americans suffered and died during World War II.

Thus, despite feeling violated as both a Muslim and an American on that day, Roxana could not ignore the fact that the U.S. was involved in just as much, if not more, exploitation around the world as it was humanitarianism. "There is no excuse for ignorance," she explains, "and nationalism dressed up as patriotism is no exception. I am proud to be American. I am proud to be Iranian. But that doesn't mean that I'm proud of everything the American and the Iranian governments do and support."

Roxana's sentiments exemplify a collective predicament in which Iranian Americans often find themselves. My father once put it this way: We are like the children of divorced parents, who love both of them equally but who, when it comes to taking sides, tend to come to the defense of the weaker party. In the case of Iranian Americans, that weaker party is generally Iran, given the wide disparities in economic power and resources. Iranian Americans tend to be a proud and stubborn bunch, brimming with contradictions.

I remember staying with Roxana at her parents' house in Orange, Connecticut, one night when they were throwing a small "gathering"—it's only a party if more than fifty people show up—for about twenty guests, mostly family friends. At the time, her parents were throwing many such "gatherings" because her dad, normally a less-than-social mathematics professor, was planning a big charity fundraiser for the earthquake victims in Bam, Iran. As a result of the December 26, 2003, earthquake, more than 43,000 people were killed, an estimated 30,000 people were injured, and up to 75,000 people were left homeless.[1]

Nearing midnight, Roxana's dad came into the family room (where we were hiding and watching *Real World* reruns) and pulled a book from the shelves in the corner of the room. Roxana immediately began pleading, "No, please no." "What is it?" I asked her, and before she could answer, I saw the book myself and immediately understood. It was a giant book of poems by Hafiz (a fourteenth-century Persian Sufi mystic who wrote largely about love and the Divine). Our poetry is sung, not read, and when I say sung, I mean *emoted*—complete with moans and other indecipherable visceral sounds. The word for "poem" and "song" in Farsi is, in fact, one and the same: *sheher*. I am not a big fan of poetry in general, but I adore Hafiz.

Still, reading poetry aloud is an art in Iran. Some are good at it, and others just lack the talent. There are literally people whose job it is to recite verse aloud at various gatherings—weddings, funerals, whatever. The woman who would be sharing her vocal stylings that evening, however, was far from a professional. Nevertheless, she was convinced that she was fantastic at it, and despite knowing better, everyone just let her sing and feigned delight at the cacophony. That night, I understood this insanity for the first time: to deny anyone the opportunity to sing Hafiz is sacrilege. His poetry is like a birthright for all Iranians. And if we want to sing, no one can stop us.

Roxana, like many Iranians, admits that she considers the great Sufi poets to be some of the finest interpreters of the Qur'an. Still, having spent her childhood living under the rule of the painfully un-Islamic "Islamic Republic of Iran," she maintains a strong residual association between faith and overly stringent directives. For example, while attending elementary school in Iran, Roxana was taught that if she failed to bend to an exact ninety-degree angle or to stand perfectly straight during certain parts of her formal prayers, then God would reject them. While she recognizes the inane and un-Islamic reasoning behind such directives, the lessons of her early religious education still haunt her. It turns out that such misguided teachings are not entirely peculiar to Iranians.

Roxana has encountered unthinkable grief since our initial interview—a grief that is far too clear and consuming to ignore. Her younger brother and only sibling, Farid, was killed in an unimaginable accident in April 2006, and when I flew in to Connecticut the next day to see her, I had no idea what to expect. Nothing can prepare you for something as gruesome and unnatural as having to watch a loving mother and father bury their only son. Roxana was visibly hysterical when I first arrived, and watching her made me truly question for the first time the Qur'anic assurance that God will never subject any human soul to a burden that is greater than it can bear (2:286, 7:42). The week I spent with Roxana's family after Farid's death was without a doubt the most unbearable of *my* life, and he wasn't even my son or my brother. I can't even begin to imagine or comprehend what Roxana or her parents must have been going through, and when I tried, I was immediately overcome with severe nausea.

True to form, Roxana did not repress an ounce of her emotion, despite everyone's efforts (including my own) to shut her up. I had rationalized my attempts to "control" her by telling myself and her that she had to pull herself together for the sake of her parents, that she had to be the calm and collected one. Stoicism, however, has never been Roxana's style, and despite everyone else's efforts, Roxana grieved the loss of her only brother in the same way she has done everything else in her life: with unfettered emotion and absolute authenticity. There is no place for proper social etiquette on such an occasion, and Roxana appeared to be the only one there who had figured this out. She took it upon herself to stand up in front of everyone at the funeral home and ask that we share any stories or memories that we had about Farid. Despite her seemingly uncontrollable emotions, she was able to oversee this event, and when it came down to it, she was ultimately the only one who could truly console and comfort her parents—which she did perfectly and effortlessly.

I began to recognize this distinctly feminine power of Roxana's for the first time at the funeral home, and I also remember very clearly that the only people who were not trying to "control" her emotion for the sake of etiquette, custom, decorum, or whatever-you-want-to-call-it were her parents. They were completely at ease with Roxana's overt and unapologetic expression of her grief. In fact, looking back on it, my sense is that they took comfort in her refusal to stay calm and rational when something so obviously violent and irrational had just taken place.

Roxana's refusal to conform to other people's skewed notions of proper social etiquette ultimately turned out to be the most rational response in hindsight, and I bear sincere regret and embarrassment at any of my efforts to curtail her natural instincts. She was in fact, in many instances, the only fully sane and sentient person in the room, and that can be so scary for other people that it's no wonder we were all trying to control *her*. What better way to distract ourselves from our own discomfort and distress? I can't think of a more selfish or more human reaction.

In the car on the way to the funeral home, Roxana was demanding very specific answers from us. She wanted to know exactly where Farid's soul was at the moment, exactly what would happen to him after the funeral, exactly what she could do to help him from where she was. None of us had any decent answers. A Pakistani friend of hers, however, who was driving the car, tried his best to answer her questions, given his personal and highly textual understandings of the Qur'an and the hadiths. This attempt at religiosity was perhaps the only thing that managed to calm Roxana down, no matter how few the answers, and for that I was supremely grateful to our driver. Still, I knew that there were no clear answers that we as mortals could fully understand, but I was willing to buy into anything at that point that appeared to offer Roxana even an iota of relief. And simply the mention of the Qur'an provided such solace for her. She kept commenting on how she couldn't imagine how anyone without faith, without Islam even, could ever endure something so horrible. Perhaps Roxana's early religious teachings in Iran were not quite so useless. Sometimes strict and absolute adherence to ritual, no matter how seemingly absurd or ungrounded, is useful. Sometimes that's all that keeps us afloat in the face of disaster.

〃〃 ﹨﹨﹨

When asked what makes a good Muslim, Roxana has little doubt. When asked whether she is one, however, she begins to waiver. She does not pray regularly, but she does pray, and she has prayed regularly during certain periods of her life. She does not wear *hijab*, but she abstains from pork and alcohol. She tries to fast during Ramadan but isn't always successful. She tries to give food or money to the poor whenever she has extra, but she is currently pretty deeply in debt from NYU tuition and the cost of living on Manhattan for five years. She openly admits that during certain periods in her life, she has doubted her faith, but she maintains that she has come back each time on her own terms and feels that her faith has only gotten stronger as a result. Since Farid's death, moreover, she seems to be clinging more strongly to her faith than ever, not simply as a means of making sense of the world but as a means of staying connected to her brother.

Roxana firmly believes that the most she can do to be a good Muslim is to be kind to other people. Her grandmother, a four-foot-eleven, ninety-pound, bitingly sarcastic woman, who still lives in the small town of Shahrood, in northern Iran, has had a huge influence on Roxana and her image of what characterizes a good Muslim. Roxana quotes her as if she were a prophet: "God can forgive us for everything we do against him, but he cannot forgive us for what we do against other people—only those people can forgive us for that." Roxana lives strictly by this mantra. She goes out of her way not to hurt people, even if it means hurting herself. She has an extremely maternal and protective instinct, and yet, there is still something distinctly childlike about her. She has absolutely no shame about being exactly who she is at all times—whether this means doing cartwheels in the frozen-food section of Stop & Shop at two o'clock in the morning, plucking her eyebrows on the subway, or asking total strangers for anything from a stick of gum to a maxipad to a brief recap of what she missed upon arriving late for a movie.

At Wesleyan, Roxana majored in neuroscience, and since I've known her, she has always been torturing animals for the sake of scientific progress and a paycheck. The year after she graduated from Wesleyan, she got a job working in a lab at Yale. As part of the job, she injected mice with some substance that completely destroyed their immune systems so that she could study deficient immune responses, among other things. I still don't fully understand what the objective was, but I do have a distinct and vivid memory of her getup every time she had to enter the "mouse room." Because all the mice were so immune-deficient, she had to wear this big white suit and helmet-looking thing every time she went in there. She looked like she was preparing to clean up toxic nuclear waste, when all she was doing was checking up on some unlucky mice.

There is something inherently attractive about Roxana, and it has nothing to do with the way her jet black hair highlights her porcelain skin and classic Persian features. I am at a loss for words to describe it, but I know I'm not the only one who sees it. Kids love her. I imagine it's because they can see that part of her that refuses to be "adult" about everything, and they still appreciate it. More than that, though, I expect it's because they feel safe and happy with her around. She is extremely aware of her surroundings and insanely protective of those closest to her, whether emotionally or spatially, especially if they are small. Like a child, Roxana is resilient and quick to forgive, and more than anyone I have ever known, she has a dangerous capacity for love. A capacity that leads me to simultaneously warn and envy her in equal parts.

One afternoon, I skipped classes and drove up to New Haven in the middle of the week to pay her a surprise visit. When I entered her lab, I was met with this bouncing white blob (complete with helmet and all) dancing and singing "Go West" at the top of her lungs with the Pet Shop Boys as backup, and instead of stopping to turn down the music or salvage some shred of decorum, she just took my hand and made me start dancing with her, as if we were at a club and she had been waiting for me. She is definitely on a different plane than the rest of us. Things are just a little louder, a little brighter, a little happier when she is in the room.

THREE

Matthew

With God are the keys
Of the Unseen, the treasures
That none knoweth but He.
He knoweth whatever there is
On the earth and in the sea.
Not a leaf doth fall
But with His knowledge:
There is not a grain
In the darkness (or the depths)
Of the earth, nor anything
Fresh or dry (green or withered),
But is (inscribed) in a Record
Clear (to those who can read).

—QUR'AN, AL AN'AM (THE CATTLE), 6:59

Seize the moment of excited curiosity on any subject to solve
your doubts; For if you let it pass, the desire may never
return, and you may remain in ignorance.

—WILLIAM WIRT, FROM JOHN PENDLETON KENNEDY,
MEMOIRS OF THE LIFE OF WILLIAM WIRT

When I finally sit Matthew down on the couch in the living room for an interview, he already knows way too much about the book. He doesn't want to do the interview and implores me to just let him answer my questions in writing. I tell him I want his gut reactions, body language, and facial expressions; I tell him I'm not interested in his intellectual analysis. He sighs and sinks into the couch, sipping his steaming cup of Darjeeling.

When I first met Matthew, I was in the process of researching the big tobacco lawsuits of the late 1990s for a government class. He tells me now that he had already been admiring me from afar for a couple of months when he saw me in the library that rainy October morning. I had never noticed him before, though. When I got up to leave, I had no idea that he had followed me out. I started walking back to my dorm, and when I had nearly made it, the boy ran up beside me and tried to casually fall into step with me. He looked anything but casual. In fact, he scared the hell out of me, but before I could reach for my pepper spray, he rushed to make his case: "I've never done this before, but I've noticed you around, and I'm super attracted to you." By this point, I was thinking, *Who is this freak, how could he really think he could lure a girl over the age of twelve using words like "super," and how stupid does he think I am?* But I was too alarmed to say anything or move.

He continued: "Where are you from?" Still startled, I blurted, "Ohio," jetting my eyes across the courtyard to see if maybe there was someone, *anyone*, I knew who could save me. When I finally looked at his face, he looked perplexed, and I added, "I'm Iranian." He told me that he thought I was Puerto Rican and that his best friend at school, Roxana, was Iranian as well. This connection suddenly made him far less threatening and gave me reason to back off the pepper spray for the moment. I'm glad I didn't attack him. For one thing, he introduced me to Roxana, whom I swiftly stole as my *own* best friend. And for another, I ended up marrying him some five years later.

I would never have guessed that a white American kid from upstate New York could ever understand, let alone interest me. I always thought that I would end up marrying a first-generation something—whether Iranian or Peruvian or Korean didn't really matter, but I was sure I'd never end up marrying what I considered to be a standard American white boy. It took knowing Matthew for me to learn, however, that there is no such thing as a standard American anything. We are a nation of anomalies.

✐✐✐ ❯❯❯

Matthew grew up some two hours north of New York City, in the heart of the Catskill Mountains, amid one of the largest Russian Jewish immigrant populations in the country. He was brought up in the Catholic Church and went to Mass on Sundays. He was the quarterback on his junior- and senior-year high-school varsity football teams, a near straight-A student, the star of the track team, and voted "most likely to succeed" by his senior class. To be completely accurate, he was apparently voted both "most athletic" *and* "most likely to succeed," and he was told that he had to pick one: he opted for the latter.

I would have absolutely hated him in high school. Apart from the good grades, we shared very little in common, and to be precise, we didn't even share that in common, as my public high school was much larger and more privileged than his. I took mostly honors and Advanced Placement classes, which meant that I got a lot of H's, meaning scoring between 90 and 100 on a five-point honors scale. Apparently, H's weren't an option at his school. While Matthew was choosing between most likely to succeed and most athletic, I— with my H's, my general disdain for the whole concept of high school, my hatred for athletics, my love for speech and debate, and my anything-but-cool ventures in social activism—was voted "most likely to take over the world."

While some might consider this comparable to the "most likely to succeed" title, I had the very clear impression that it was meant more as a jab at my activism than as a genuine positive predictor of success, as I was always trying to raise money or awareness about some country or region of the world that no one had ever heard of or cared to think about.

Meanwhile, Matthew managed to cast his first vote for Bob Dole, while I proudly sported my Clinton-Gore "Building a Bridge to the 21st Century" T-shirt all over the place, being just a year too young to vote. I have little doubt that if Matthew and I had ever crossed paths in high school, we would have been arch-nemeses. Fortunately, however, we didn't, and by the time we met, Matthew was just as embarrassed by his vote for Dole as I was by my former blind devotion to the power letter-writing campaigns might hold over ruthless military dictators.

In college, Matthew traded track and football for squash and tae kwon do. He majored in economics and Russian and East European studies. Having grown up in the "Borsch Belt," surrounded by so many Russian immigrants, Matthew had an American experience that was also very much a distinctly Eastern European one, so I assume his Russian studies immersion reminded him of home. At school, he lived in the Russian House with mostly native

Russkies, learned to speak Russian, studied Russian history and literature, almost exclusively dated Russian girls, and draped a giant Soviet flag over the closet door of his upstairs room. He spent his summers traveling to Russia, first to Siberia with his childhood friend Chris, and then to Moscow and St. Petersburg alone. Matthew was, and remains, a bona-fide Russophile.

In hindsight, he insists that he chose to so immerse himself in Russian culture because he didn't feel as if he had his own distinct culture. He says now that he thought this immersion would help him gain a clear and distinguishable identity, but he admits that it did nothing of the sort. No matter how much Russian history he learned or vodka he drank, he would still be an American. After realizing this, Matthew claims, he began to sober up and see that the reason that his identity as an American was not clear and easily definable was because America itself is not clear and easily definable.

Matthew's mother, Jean, is in fact British, but she became an American citizen nearly twenty years ago. She came to New York at the age of nineteen on the *Queen Mary*. She met Matthew's dad, Tom, a first-generation American who was born and raised in Brooklyn by Slovenian immigrants, when they were both working at the same midtown Manhattan bank. Because not every American comes from the same British and Slovenian background, or is brought up surrounded by the same Russian émigré community, it was difficult for Matthew to understand what exactly it was that made him American at all. Today, he still has trouble explaining what being an American means to him, but he has no trouble admitting that he is American by more than mere circumstance of birth or geography, and that he is exceedingly fortunate to be part of a culture that would not exist but for the abundance of distinct diasporas within it.

⸝⸝⸝ ⟩⟩⟩

During Matthew's senior year in college, my junior year, we lived next door to each other. His romantic pursuit of me two years earlier had failed miserably after his overzealous approach and introduction, but unlike any of the other boys I met during that first year in college, he was the only one who genuinely tried to be friends with me after I told him that I did not want to be anyone's "girlfriend" and that I would not kiss him, let alone sleep with him.

Matthew had spent the previous year in London, studying at the London School of Economics, and I had spent that same year in and out of the hospital. I missed the spring semester to finally have surgery to remove my pancreatic tumor. It was around this time that I began going through a serious depression. Meanwhile, Matthew kept writing me letters and calling me from London.

He and Roxana were my only friends from college who kept in touch with me during that year. I can't remember ever feeling more weak and hopeless. Each time I heard from Matthew, he reminded me that he thought I was one of the strongest people he'd ever met. He told me that this was obvious from the way I walked. He told me that my long upright strides were not just a way to get from here to there, but a silent message to the rest of the world that I was not a woman to be messed with. He told me that everyone who saw me walk past could see my strength and that he didn't believe for a second that I couldn't find it. He was right not to believe this: I could find it, and with his steady encouragement, I did.

When I ask Matthew what brought him to Islam, he says I did. When I ask myself what brought me to Islam, I now realize that, in many ways, his faith in me did. When I first read the entire Qur'an, I began to find that the strength Matthew consistently reminded me of had come from my roots: despite the fact that my parents had never pushed Islam on me and were not overtly religious themselves, I found that I had unknowingly enjoyed a very solid Muslim upbringing in the basic tenets of Islam. All the lessons that my parents had taught me by both example and tutelage were present in the Qur'an, and the fundamental moral attitudes we shared in common were all buttressed in the Qur'anic text. Matthew, then, brought me back to my faith by reminding me of a visceral strength, grounded in my heritage and upbringing, which I had forgotten I possessed.

✦✦✦ ❭❭❭

Matthew's path to Islam was far less straightforward and predictable. Not having a Muslim upbringing or any knowledge of the religion's essence until his early adulthood, Matthew truly *chose* Islam. Unlike the many who consider themselves Muslim only because they were raised by Muslims parents, Matthew considers himself Muslim solely because Islam enriches his life and improves his person. He is a very sensible and studious person. He loves to read, and he is more impressed by logic and good sense than by eloquent rhetoric.

Matthew is a public school teacher in inner-city Atlanta. He shares few experiences in common with his students, mostly underprivileged African American adolescents from single-parent families, but he insists that he wouldn't want to be teaching anyone else. "They teach me as much as I teach them. They don't dress things up like adults do. They tell it how it is, even though how it is isn't so great for them right now. I'll never fully understand how hard it is for some of my kids, but I can't ignore that no matter what their situation is, so many of them are so obviously ten times smarter than your average white middle-class kid who doesn't have to worry about anything other than soccer practice or video games. There's wisdom that comes with loss and sacrifice at such a young age, and if they can turn it around the right way, I'm telling you, these kids can change the world. How could I not want to be even the tiniest part of that?"

In response to being asked why he chose Islam, Matthew, being the well-prepared teacher that he is, presents an arsenal of different rational responses —perhaps because he has had to answer this same question so many times for wide-eyed, incredulous audiences. He begins by telling me that he chose Islam because he never believed in the concept of vicarious redemption through the suffering of Christ and because he could never accept that someone could be damned just because he or she wasn't baptized into a particular church or religion. He chose Islam because it does not reject anyone from the possibility of deliverance on account of anything other than his or her actions and intentions. He chose Islam because nowhere in the Qur'an does it say that if he didn't, he would be doomed to eternal damnation. Finally, he tells me that he chose Islam because it appealed to his logic and his sensibilities and because, despite its manipulation for self-serving, fundamentalist political ends around the world, it is a religion that does not endorse hierarchical structures of study or practice.

Conversion is a distinctive and extraordinary way to come to any religion. Converting to Islam requires saying and believing, first, that there is only one God and, second, that there is no God other than Him (the same God of the Jewish and Christian traditions) and that Muhammad is His prophet.* While Matthew believes and has repeated these words many times, and while he correctly calls himself a Muslim, as a convert he still considers his passage to Islam an ongoing process—so much so that several times during our interview, he tells me that maybe someone else would be a better choice, maybe a better convert, someone who has already started to practice, he says. I have no doubt, however, that he is a fine example of a good Muslim and a dedicated convert;

---

*In Arabic, this statement is called the *shahada,* and it is transliterated into the euphonic "La ilaha il Allah, Muhammad-ur-Rasool-Allah."

the fact that he has just recently and somewhat sporadically started praying and fasting only reinforces this. He refuses to practice anything unless he knows exactly why he is doing it and what it means, and his insistence on attaining and maintaining pure intentions is in accordance with Islam, as the Qur'an and the hadiths consistently preach that actions are not judged according to their completion or results even but rather according to the intentions that underlie them. Doing the right thing for the wrong reason is indeed a serious offense in Islam (see 33:5), and it is an offense that Matthew is absolutely vigilant about avoiding.

Matthew's explanation for his initial delay in formal practice after his conversion reminds me of the day of Julie's wedding. Julie was a friend of mine from college, and she got married in Central Park while Matthew and I were still living in New York. It was a beautiful day, and the Jewish/Protestant ceremony went off without a hitch. The bride was stunning, and her and her new husband's obvious joy was infectious. After the ceremony, Matthew and I decided to walk around the Upper East Side, still in our dress clothes. He was wearing a shirt and tie, and I was wearing a sleeveless cerulean sundress. As we walked past the mosque on the corner of Ninety-sixth Street and Third Avenue, Matthew said he wanted to go in and buy this Qur'an translated by Abdullah Yusuf Ali that he was sure they had there. I was skeptical. I told him that I didn't mind if he went in, but that I would wait outside because I didn't really feel like going in and besides, I knew that I was dressed inappropriately for the occasion.

Apparently, while I was waiting outside, the men at the mosque started preparing Matthew to pray—showing him how to wash his hands and feet. He told me it all happened so quickly and was all so hurried and unfamiliar that he didn't know what to do. The whole time he kept asking if he could have a chador to bring out to me so that I could come in, but no one paid any attention to his request. They insisted that he start praying in Arabic, since he happened to come in during afternoon prayers, and when Matthew told them that he didn't understand what he was saying, they told him that it didn't matter. At this point, he got up and left. As he was leaving, one of the "brothers" saw him and told him that he should make me dress more modestly.

Matthew came out livid. While he hadn't even yet converted at that point, he was already fairly knowledgeable about the faith and was growing increasingly cynical about the prospect of Islamic brotherhood. He told me that he couldn't believe that these people who were supposed to be so religious seemed to know nothing about Islam. I wasn't surprised. I have found that this kind of behavior and ignorance within the "Muslim" community make it much harder to be a Muslim American than any ignorance or prejudice from the non-Muslim community. I never overtly encouraged Matthew to become a Muslim, and I really didn't expect that he would. I was just glad that he was interested in my background and beliefs.

When he started talking about converting, I grew immediately nervous. What would his family think? What would my family think? In short, I was thinking only about myself and what his decision might mean for *me*. I had yet to consider the ramifications for Matthew or the reasons behind his decision. All I kept thinking was that I would be blamed for this. I was sure that his parents would hate me. When I finally forgot about myself and got around to listening to him, though, I realized that none of this mattered and that most of my fears were unfounded, especially given the fact that everyone who truly knew Matthew also knew enough to trust his judgment in matters relating to his personal beliefs and knew he was a free thinker: not only difficult to persuade but impossible to coerce.

Despite the barrage of disappointments from both the Muslim and non-Muslim communities, which have at times been slow to understand and accept him as a tolerant and educated Muslim man, Matthew insists that he enjoys being Muslim. He especially enjoys being a convert, despite the fact that it is not uncommon for Muslims, on discovering that he is a convert, to take it upon themselves to not-so-subtly suggest how he might perfect his worship and for non-Muslims to try and win him back to a more "acceptable" creed. Being a convert, Matthew claims, he feels that he is less prone to fall victim to complacency. "In a way, I feel like I'm coming from a vulnerable position. I can't make up for not being Muslim in the past in any way other than by studying Islam now.

"I think Islam works best for me because it doesn't force me to ignore or go against human nature. For me, being Muslim means learning more about human nature and the capacities of the human spirit. Islam is still new to me. After I feel comfortable with my knowledge base and my understanding behind practices, I hope *insha'Allah* to become more observant. I think that if you have faith, knowledge is the next step, and only after knowledge should come practice. Now, I practice through studying the Qur'an and the hadiths.

"I pray in English and in my own words, and one day when I'm ready, I will learn the formal prayers, but now I'm focusing on knowledge and learning. I'm growing. Conversion is hard. It's like learning a new language. It's nearly impossible to learn to speak a language perfectly unless you're brought up speaking it. And even if you are brought up speaking it, there is still always something more to learn in terms of grammar or vocabulary. Same with Islam. It's a hard process learning about Islam, but it is worth it because it makes me happy, and I keep finding that it's true that for every step you take toward God, he takes two steps toward you. It's a process for me. I'd be kidding myself to say that I could convert into a perfect Muslim overnight."

We'd all be kidding ourselves to think that we could convert into a perfect anything overnight. Generally, the greater the goal, the more patience is required to attain it. Matthew is incredibly patient, and his patience allows his reason to preside over his emotions in circumstances that would prove impossible for me and I dare say for the great majority. People exhibit varied reactions upon finding out that Matthew is Muslim, depending on who they are. Many of those who knew him—and not so well—before his conversion falsely assume that he converted in order to marry me. But Matthew knew that all he had to do was ask.

Still, he is determinedly patient with those who insist that he must have converted as a prerequisite for marrying me, and who cannot fathom that anyone in his right mind would *choose* to become a Muslim, any more than he would choose to become a paraplegic. Matthew calmly explains his choice to these people in a slow and seemingly unperturbed manner, just as he did to me in his interview. The general response of those who meet Matthew after his conversion is similar, but in this respect, he is becoming familiar with a phenomenon that I have experienced my entire life. While I have now grown so sick and tired of it that I generally simply try to avoid and ignore it, Matthew is green and much less jaded.

When people tell me that I don't look Muslim, either because I don't wear *hijab* or because I don't fit one of their fifty preset stereotypes, I usually respond by telling them that they don't look stupid. When people tell Matthew that *he* doesn't look Muslim because of his pale skin or his bright green eyes, however, he is not so easily annoyed or flustered, and because of his patience and level-headedness, he is able to use the exchange as an opportunity to educate without the slightest degree of condescension. He says that he respects any non-Muslim who asks questions, not just because he used to be one of them but because, he says, such questions suggest the "goal of escaping ignorance." It baffles me to this day that despite being as much of a brat as I obviously am, I managed to attract someone so patient, gracious, and dignified. I guess there's no set rational formula for taste, attraction, or providence.

When I reach the end of my interview with Matthew, it is nearing two o'clock in the morning. He is lying on the couch petting our fat black cat, Olyan, who is purring ridiculously loudly and nudging his head into Matthew's chin. He seems to have noticed Matthew's unease before I have and is already trying to quell it when I first take note of the look of distress on my husband's face. I ask him what's wrong, and he says, "I feel like you got me at a bad time. I'm just becoming a Muslim—I'm so early in the process." The truth is that I couldn't have caught him at a better time. We are all constantly in the course of becoming ourselves, and it is only through this endless series of transitions that we can come to understand ourselves and one another.

FOUR

Ameer

And among God's Signs
Is the creation of the heavens
And the earth, and the variations
In your languages
And your colors; verily
In that are Signs
For those who know.

And among His Signs
Is the sleep that ye take
By night and by day,
And the quest that ye
(Make for livelihood)
Out of His Bounty: verily
In that are Signs
For those who hearken.

And among His Signs,
He shows you the lightning,
By way both of fear
And of hope, and He sends
Down rain from the sky
And with it gives life to
The earth after it is dead:
Verily in that are Signs
For those who are wise.

And among His Signs is this,
That heaven and earth
Stand by His Command:
Then when He calls you,
By a single call, from the earth,
Behold, ye (straightway) come forth.

—QUR'AN, AL RUM (THE ROMANS), 30:22–25

If ya ain't got it in ya, ya can't blow it out.

—LOUIS ARMSTRONG

Ameer was very nearly the last person I expected to meet in the course of writing this book. He fit none of the categories I had set out to cover. His very existence precluded even an attempt at categorization.

Ameer is what some might call a very "by-the-book" Muslim. He prays five times a day; he fasts; he aims to keep and respect each of the five pillars literally. Still, he insists that he observes in this way because he thinks he is not as spiritually gifted as some others, who may be able to reach the same ends without the same rigorous practice. While Ameer is just as observant and knowledgeable as the many religious leaders and figureheads I have encountered, he has none of their airs of moral superiority or presumptuousness. He looks to Islam as a guide, and it works for him. As for everyone else, he maintains, "Whatever works for them, if that moves 'em on in the world, you know? God bless 'em. Let 'em do their thing, yo."

Ameer insists, moreover, that he is "only possible in America." By this, he does not mean that a Korean woman and an Egyptian man could not have met, married, and had a family anywhere else. "That could have happened anywhere," he says. "As a biracial," he explains, "I am being raised in a language that is neither of my parents' native languages. What I've become is only possible in America, and I don't think I could live anywhere else."

Ameer grew up in a rich suburb just outside of Cleveland, where he attended private school. When I first met him, he was in the middle of his junior year at Yale, where he was majoring in film. His older brother and sister both went to Princeton, so he was in his own way a bit of a rebel. When we first met, Ameer told me that he "eventually" wanted to teach, "probably high school, maybe English." Today "eventually" has become reality.

Ameer is now living in Washington Heights and teaching tenth-graders in the South Bronx at a small public high school called the Bronx Academy of Letters. He spent his first year after graduation, however, teaching high-school English on a Native American reservation in New Mexico. Despite not having an ounce of Native American blood in his body, Ameer feels strangely and strongly drawn to Native American cultures. He explains this seemingly peculiar attraction as a form of respect for his ancestry, an assertion that is initially highly confusing, given Ameer's lack of Native American lineage and his admittedly privileged, though culturally diverse, upbringing.

More than anything else, Ameer is an American. While his Americanness is the direct result of a more modern cultural construction of the postcolonial American "melting pot" or "salad bowl," Ameer is not culturally capable of ignoring the embarrassing history of the inception of this country he calls home. Being a minority within a minority, Ameer relates deeply to the process of the dissipation of culture and the struggle to maintain some sort of unified identity, more than he relates to any one particular Korean or Egyptian tradition. Herein lies much of the source of Ameer's attraction to Native American cultures; he cannot help but appreciate Native American struggles, for he has been confronting similar struggles on a very personal level his entire life. Ameer's respect for and connection to Native American cultures, thus, lies not in his blood or his upbringing but in his beliefs and his understandable struggle for identity.

Ameer speaks like no one I've ever met. His voice and his words have such a rhythm and musicality about them that at times he sounds as if he's swallowed a metronome. In fact, upon taking just a few moments to really *listen* to his speech patterns, it becomes immediately clear that Ameer tends to speak, quite naturally and inadvertently, in song. During our interview, he mentioned a small rap group that he and his cousins had put together—a Muslim hip-hop group called The Desert Crew. I thought it was cute and comical at first, and he was so flippant about it that I didn't pay serious attention at the time. Weeks after our first encounter, however, I received a CD in the mail entitled *Facing East*. On the back was a picture of Ameer and two other kids about the same age. It looked so professional—shrink-wrapped and everything.

Still, I was more than a little afraid that it would suck. What would I say to him if I absolutely hated it? What if it was so cheesy that it prevented me from writing honestly without him hating me? What if it changed my impression of him entirely? So at first, I listened to it with extreme fear and hesitation. Given the dynamic and multifaceted person Ameer is, I would have been happy and able to write his chapter with a clear conscience if his music was just decent—anything short of lousy would have been good enough for me, in the absence of any unforgivable cheese. If the CD was just decent, I could still respect him and write about all the other facets of his life and personality without focusing too much on Ameer: the rapper.

Listening to the album, however, particularly the tracks that Ameer (aka Qwazimoto, Quazy, Aboriginal, Aborij) wrote, I was blown away. I have never listened to any music that made me more proud to be who I am—more proud to be Muslim, more proud to be the child of immigrants, more proud to pray, more proud to believe, and, no joke, more proud to be from Ohio—and to top it off, the music, the rapping, the timing, the quality: all of it was stellar.

That first week I got it, Matthew nearly hid it from me because it was all that I would listen to. I learned all the lyrics within a few days and began singing along. Cruising the streets of Atlanta with my windows open and the stereo blasting, I felt like an obnoxious high-schooler who had just gotten her license, but I didn't care. I was loving it.

Ameer tells his story in song on the album, and although his is definitely a unique and completely individual story, I found it highly relatable. Listening to his raps only confirmed my speculation that Ameer was indeed the most truly American individual I had ever met.

> I'm the gray ghost, neither black nor white
> Neither wack nor tight because I lack the sight
> To see anything, as either one or the other
> In many ways I'm in between my father and mother
> . . . I'm America, the real America not the bully
> Tryin' to stay independent of the devils that pull me
> In directions of violence and anger. . . .
> —From "Sh-t That Quazy Wrote"*

I first heard about Ameer through the head of the Muslim Students Association (MSA) at Yale, whom I contacted because I had communicated with the Yale MSA several times in the past, as the leader of Wesleyan's MSA, and I knew that the group was fairly strong.† I was headed to Wesleyan for another interview anyway and thought it might be worth making the half-hour drive to Yale if I could find someone worth interviewing there. After hearing only a little bit about Ameer, I had found more than enough reason.

Having never encountered anyone of half-Korean, half-Egyptian descent, I wasn't quite sure what to expect. We arranged to meet at the Au Bon Pain on the corner of Broadway and York, which was very familiar to me, given that I had worked as a salesclerk at a jewelry shop only a few stores down for nearly a year not long before. He told me that he looked Puerto Rican, which I found amusing given that I too am often mistaken as such—so much so that I

---

*These lyrics and those that follow are taken from The Desert Crew album *Facing East*. All the cited lyrics were written by Ameer and are available at the Web site http://www.the desertcrew.com., along with information about the band's upcoming tours and albums.

†Wesleyan's MSA was not part of the national MSA when I was running it. I am uncertain as to the Wesleyan MSA's current status or the former or current affiliations of the Yale MSA.

learned Spanish solely for the purpose of understanding what the total strangers who spoke to me, assuming that I was Hispanic, were saying. I found out later that Ameer had done so for the same reason.

I had been waiting for a couple of minutes when I noticed a group in the corner laughing and speaking Arabic. After a while, I approached one of them and asked him if he was half Korean, and he let out a deafening laugh. Apparently not. He told me that they were all speaking Arabic, not Korean. I just left their table, not being in the mood to explain. Shortly thereafter, Ameer walked in and came right up to me and shook my hand. I had informed him only that I was brown-haired, -skinned, and -eyed, and that I would be wearing a leopard-fur-trimmed collar, which I guess was sufficient.

Because he was fasting for Ramadan, we decided to change location. We headed to the Barnes and Noble down the street and took up residence in the café for the next few hours. He didn't require much explanation from me. He understood what I was doing, and he wasn't shy, so although we spent only a short time in each other's actual *physical* presence, we were able to immediately get past small talk and other such bullshitting to use our time to try to connect and understand one another. Miraculously, I think we did—although three years of staying in touch since haven't hurt either.

Ameer grew up in a predominantly wealthy and elderly Jewish neighborhood in an eastern suburb of Cleveland called Pepper Pike. His parents met when they were both interns at Cleveland's Marymount Hospital. His mom is now a psychiatrist, and his dad is an obstetrician-gynecologist. "Typical FOB [fresh off the boat] story," Ameer explains. "They came with nothing and then started making money, met, got married, and moved to the suburbs, you know?" I knew all too well. I almost felt like he was telling me my own story. Having also grown up in Ohio as the child of two physicians—my father also an ob-gyn—I felt a fairly instant connection with Ameer.

Partly, our connection was the result of what I call the COFOB (children of fresh off the boats) connection. There exists a strong sense of compassion and camaraderie among COFOBs growing up in America, regardless of origin: the sense that we need to make something of ourselves because our parents worked and gave up so much to give us this privileged life, the ability to adapt quickly to new people and environments, the inclination to always see things from at least two sides, the inability to fully communicate with our parents because we literally speak different languages, and the tendency to experience the present as a constant reminder of our dissipating pasts. Thus, in many ways,

Ameer

it was the COFOB connection, more so than the mere Muslim connection, that I think allowed Ameer and me to be so immediately open and honest with one another. Being a COFOB is an incredibly distinct experience, and in some ways, it takes one to know one.

I was brought up, for example, with a sense (not uncommon among immigrant diasporas with long and celebrated histories of civilization) that Americans have no culture; that they are completely devoid of any of the spice or originality that any culture requires; that they are just confused imperialists who think they are better than everyone else but have no solid explanation as to why. Now, I realize that American culture thrives on this absence of any single unitary culture. It is, at its very essence, in fact, a COFOB culture. As COFOBs, we are constantly being asked where we are from, and then where we are *really* from. Constantly explaining and justifying one's identity and origin is a hallmark of the COFOB experience. Every day, without fail, I hear some variation of the where-are-you-from question, and the only consistency is that my response is always inconsistent. Sometimes I say Iran, sometimes I say America, sometimes I say Dayton, and sometimes I lie—saying I am from someplace I anticipate my interrogator has never heard of, like Tuvalu or Swaziland. It's easy to get tired of strangers assuming you don't belong. I understand where Ameer is coming from.

> Why oh why oh, did I ever leave Ohio?
> Now I'm feelin' every last one of these 532 miles
> Damn my style so Ohio
> But I'm falooka, that mean I'm lost in denial
> . . . But I'm not full Korean and not full Egyptian
> And not bein' full anything is not efficient
> So when people ask me where I'm from I'll
> Just smile, and tell 'em that I'm from Ohio
> Where Friday nights is a football thing
> And everything else is huh ya'll thing
> The towns is segregated, and everybody hate it
> I'm a raceless face, and yet I made it
> And I'm a go back, like a Jim Brown throwback
> Aborij been down and ya'll know that
> I've learned my lesson, ask me if I ever leave the O-h-ten again

Ameer

I respond with a no way my friend, I been two-one-six
[Ameer's Cleveland area code].

—From "Ohio"

Of being at Yale, Ameer insists that he had been "dislocated" to New Haven and that eventually he wants to live closer to his family again. Still, he claims that he doesn't consider home a place but a collection of people. He speaks of his family, particularly his mother, with the same careful respect, concern, and humility he uses when he speaks of his devotion to Islam. When he talks about the Prophet Muhammad, Ameer's voice takes on a tone of purpose and direction that I rarely witness in my peers. "Men need to learn about being men. They need to learn to step up and take responsibility. The Prophet Muhammad treated everyone with respect, and he took care of business."

So when I kneel I'm askin' for Allah to hear and heal

All of the painful memories Ameer can feel

That post in the back of my mind

Askin' for rhymes to express the reason for my action and times. . . .

—From "Cry Tender"

For Ameer, being Muslim entails striving to be positive, strong, helpful, and kind. He has never considered not being Muslim, and he also can't imagine marrying a non-Muslim girl: "I don't want someone to try to convert me—no matter how subtle. I feel like it's very difficult to be a Muslim woman in America—especially now." When I ask him about his views on today's Muslim American community on the whole, he is quick to shun any sort of generalizations: "I can only talk about what I've experienced—you know? My life in Cleveland, where there's a huge African American and Palestinian [Muslim] community and a small Pakistani and Arab [Muslim] community, where my dad was president of the Islamic Center and where I went to Montessori school and then to private school after that. I can't just generalize, but I can tell you what I think." After some encouragement and a few more qualifiers about how he can only speak for himself, Ameer agrees to tell me what he thinks, so long as I make it clear that it is only what *he* thinks and that he's not trying to speak for anyone else.

"I think we just got some reorganizing to do. . . . I think we need to learn to deal with ourselves first and foremost. I mean, if your insides are messed up—like if you have cancer or something—getting plastic surgery ain't gonna help you none." I never quite thought of it in those terms, but upon hearing Ameer's analogy, I understand straightaway what he is getting at. There are those within the Muslim community who focus so much on the external appearance of others that they fail to even begin to consider the status of their own souls. Indeed, this hypocrisy is apparent within many communities, but with respect to the Muslim American community, it has had particularly disastrous effects.

For example, I have more than once been accosted by fellow Muslims—total strangers—telling me that I should cover my hair, or telling my husband that *he* should make me cover my hair, or telling me that my prayers are all for naught because I have polish on my toes or traces of mascara on my lashes. Such behaviors from within the Muslim community have done more than misinform: they have convinced many of those born into Muslim families that their ancestors maintain similarly backward, shallow, and/or misogynistic beliefs.

Ameer is right when he says that it must be hard to be a Muslim woman in America today. But for me, it is not so hard because of the ignorance or prejudice of non-Muslims. It is harder because I often find that those within my own community would rather talk to me about the alcohol content in my tiramisu or the inappropriate nature of my attire than about the beautiful and essential teachings of the Holy Qur'an. Such trivial debates, literally over something as ridiculous as nail polish, can last hours and, in the end, leave both parties even further from truth, beauty, faith, or anything meaningful than they were to begin with. By focusing on these superficial indicia, it is easy to end up forgetting that "(What counts is) the intention of your hearts, and God is Oft-Forgiving, Most Merciful" (33:5).

♦♦♦ ❯❯❯

During the course of our discussion, Ameer asks me whether my parents are religious. I respond almost instinctively: "No, not really. You know, they drink, and they don't really fast or pray." In turn, Ameer asks me why I choose to reduce faith to such a tiresome set of directives, which is so odd and refreshing to hear coming from someone as observant as Ameer. "It's more than just a bunch of rules. I mean, maybe those rules work or help, but there's so much more to it than that. You can't just reduce Islam to just a bunch of rules." Internalizing the fact that I still harbor some of the misconceptions about Islam that I'm attempting to destroy is disconcerting at best.

Ameer is right though, and because I know it, I'm instantly overwhelmed by embarrassment and gratitude. Embarrassment because of the obvious hypocrisy: here I am, Miss Overenthused-purpose-driven-Muslim-writer-taking-it-upon-herself-to-vindicate-Islam-through-storytelling, trying to dispel stereotypes and get past surface illusions, all the while subconsciously contributing to these very illusions. Grateful because with that single question, Ameer inadvertently reminds me that I'm not immune to making obtuse and superficial judgments regarding the faith of others and even my own. He reminds me that understanding any experience, whether one's own or that of another, requires nothing short of determined vigilance: it requires constantly trying to step outside of oneself to see the world from a different angle, and above all, it requires sincere compassion.

> The revolution will not be televised so
> Turn off your idiot box
> If we spend so much time listenin' to CNN lyin'
> We forget it's our people overseas dyin'
> And that go for watchin' satellite too
> Our eyes ain't on the prize if our eyes is on the tube
> I know sometimes we gotta hear it from our own kind
> But the satellite is keepin' us six hours behind
>
> . . . Showdown Iraq has got play by play coverage
> Is that's what's got Muslims scared to show they face in public?
> Naw get out, get up, throw your fist up
> Show 'em we about peace and they are bound to get wit us
> Get out, get up, throw your peace sign up
> Show 'em we about peace and they'll get wit us
>
> Put your fist up, put your fist in the sky, put your fist in the sky.
> —From "Put Your Fist in the Sky"

FIVE

Sarah

Your Lord knoweth best
What is in your hearts:
If ye do deeds of righteousness,
Verily He is Most Forgiving
To those who turn to Him
Again and again.

—QUR'AN, AL ISRA' OR BANI ISRA'IL (THE NIGHT
JOURNEY OR THE CHILDREN OF ISRAEL), 17:25

I hate straight singing.
I have to change a tune to my own way of doing it.
That's all I know.

—BILLIE HOLIDAY

efore I finished asking Sarah even the most basic questions (name, age, background, core beliefs or philosophies), which had come to form the backbone of most of the interviews I had conducted up to that point, I was already high. Having never previously partaken in any sort of illicit drug use, even after four years at Wesleyan, where such "exploration" is very nearly a graduation requirement, I had no idea how I'd respond. I did, however, possess the inane, though overwhelming, conviction that in order to best serve my art and to fully understand Sarah as an individual, so as to write about her in any meaningful capacity given our short acquaintance, I would have to succumb to her reality during our time together. This reality entailed sharing the evening with Sarah's multicolored handblown glass marijuana pipe, which she had lovingly named Sheniqua, and exchanging occasional scraps of insight between unprovoked fits of laughter in the spare bedroom of the on-campus house she was sharing with her girlfriend, Lia, at the time.

When Sarah and I first crossed paths, I was for the first time in my life doing exactly what I wanted to be doing at exactly the time I wanted to be doing it, and she was comfortably waiting out the last few months of her senior year at Wesleyan with no definite future plans in sight. Of me, she knew only that I was a wannabe writer who had just dropped out of law school for the time being to pursue that fantasy, and of her, I knew only that she was a friend of a few of my old college friends and that she met the basic requirements for my book: she was Muslim, she was an American citizen, and she was relatively young.

‹‹‹ ›››

Sarah was born in Khartoum, Sudan, and lived there until the age of seven, when she left with her mom and her sister. They went to Yemen, where they lived for four years before moving to the United States. She proudly describes her parents as political activists who fought against the established Sudanese regime of their time. Her mother, who is fully Sudanese but lived in Egypt, worked for Oxfam International. Her father, who is half Sudanese and half Egyptian, was born and raised in Sudan, where he worked on agricultural pesticide-control efforts. Shortly after Sarah, her mom, and her sister left for Yemen, her father was arrested in Sudan before he could join them. He was then sent to a torture house for four months, where he underwent excruciating physical and psychological torment, including electric shock treatments. He managed to sneak out of the country after being released, and he came straight to Yemen to join the rest of his family.

Sarah was eleven when her family applied for political asylum and came to the United States, but in true COFOB style, she didn't officially obtain American citizenship until quite recently. On an early September morning, Sarah began the two-and-a-half-hour drive from Wesleyan to Boston to swear herself in and formally become an American citizen. On the way there, she crashed her 1990 Corolla into a brand-new Lexus SUV, leaving a small dent in the Lexus and totaling her Corolla. Still, she made it to the courthouse fifteen minutes before the naturalization ceremony began and was able to swear herself in.

Minutes after formally becoming an American citizen, Sarah was faced with the dilemma of how to get back to school with no car, twenty dollars in her bank account, and only two dollars and fifty cents on her person. She bummed a cigarette, bought a cup of coffee, called her girlfriend for a ride back to school, and sat waiting outside of the courthouse. Describing the events of that day, Sarah is nothing but smiles and laughs, with one exception: a hint of grief overcomes her voice as she recounts losing a large selection of audiotapes from Egypt and Sudan. "They were all in the car, and after the tow truck took it away they were just gone. And they were totally irreplaceable. I mean, they were so old and so muddled—you know, taped off the radio or off of other tapes. Horrible, horrible sound quality, but irreplaceable." Today Sarah is living in New York City, where she is in the process of recording her first full-length album, which I'm sure will not be released on audiocassette. Her debut album, produced by Nas Jota Records, is a combination of her own original songs and remixes of traditional Sudanese songs.[1]

Sarah's naturalization papers are not the sole or even the primary source of her attachment to this country, though they are the first items she mentions when I ask her how and why she sees herself as American.

"Yeah, I went through all the shit the immigration office puts you through in order to get that damned piece of paper. That makes me American, I guess. When I travel abroad and I speak English and get blamed for all the crappy foreign policies this country has, that makes me an American. When I enjoy the advantages and privileges of living in the States and being a member of the most powerful country in the world, that makes me an American. I know more about reality TV shows than is at all necessary—that also makes me an American. I mean, I can go on for hours about what makes a person an American. I don't know what being an American means.

"I consider myself an American with stipulations. I'm a *Sudanese* American, not just an American. I have multiple cultural identities and obligations to many peoples. I guess I've never sat down and defined what being an American means to me. I always associated the word *American* to be another, someone who isn't me. Even though I have American citizenship and an insane attachment and association with the fashions and subcultures that have come out of it [America] over the past fifteen years, even though I'm clearly an American fashion whore, people can't see that. Really, though, my body is historically inscribed. I'm always asked, 'Where are you from?' I know what people mean, so just to fuck with them I say, 'Well, I'm from Massachusetts,' and they'll say, 'Oh no, where are you *originally* from?' I mean, when was the last time you asked a white person or even a black person (who doesn't have an accent), 'Where are you *originally* from?'

"American culture is a culture that has many pockets in it—many subcultures in it. Other cultures are much less pocketlike. There might be dents in the fabric, but not so many pockets, and all of those pockets together have a feel and a taste to them that is American. Maybe one day they'll just get it: those pockets *are* America, and that is where I originate—*that* is where I am *really* from. You know what I mean?"

I do, and I did, but in my altered state I couldn't help but laugh hysterically at the analogy. "So you mean you aren't really from Sudan? You mean I came all the way to fucking Connecticut in the middle of fucking December to interview a girl from Pocket? Are you even Muslim, or are you part of some pagan pocket cult like everyone else at Wesleyan?" When I play back the digital recording on my laptop in the privacy of my own living room for the first time, I am mortified, not to mention incredibly annoyed at myself, in retrospect, now having to sort through seven and a half hours of giggling to find such scraps of meaningful discourse, only to hear my own idiotic responses lead the dialogue from constructive insight back to inane gibberish. Fortunately for me, Sarah was lucid enough to continue leading us back to sanity despite my incessant declarations that I wasn't normally this moronic and my constant concerned and impassioned queries as to whether I would be this stupid forever.

"Yes, Melody," she continued to reassure me. "Not to worry. I know you're smart; I promise this will wear off, and I really am Muslim." For a moment, remembering that I would be leaving Middletown the next day, I managed to muster enough acuity to ask her to elaborate on her personal commitment to Islam. For the first eight years of her formal education, she told me, Sarah took religion classes every day, and by the time she left Sudan, she had half of the Qur'an memorized. Though not saying so explicitly, Sarah made it clear that

Sarah

her greatest religious teacher and influence was her father—a statement that I would come to more fully understand over a year later, when I unknowingly ran into him and had the pleasure of his company and conversation at a Muslim conference in Atlanta. "He knows a lot about the Qur'an. He's been through a lot, and I think it's been his strength." When I ask Sarah why she considers herself Muslim, her response is firm and decisive. Her voice takes on a tone of gravity and conviction so striking that it eclipses even the tranquil mood of the room that the fog of marijuana and the faint hum of Billie Holiday pouring in from the hall stereo have so effortless combined to create.

"I consider myself Muslim because I find it to be a beautiful religion. Islam has a beautiful basic message about embracing your humanity through prayer, fasting, indulgence in *eids* [religious holidays], through accepting love and sex. It's one of the few formal religions I have come across that explicitly mentions sex positively. There is no harm in sex between married couples. I just think Islam embraces humanity. It doesn't ask anything of us that is humanly impossible. Yeah, it might be hard, but it is consistent with human nature—not contradictory to it."

Upon hearing Sarah say this, it becomes clear to me why she—someone who follows very few of the "rules" of the religion, which Ameer had so incisively cautioned me about only a day before—is so adamant about her identification with Islam. Sarah could never be an ascetic. As she puts it, "I am really into pleasure. I think being happy and in harmony with yourself and your surroundings is everyone's purpose in life. Dude, I think I'm like one of the worst Muslims I know." This last statement throws me off. "What do you mean? You seem so cool with where you're at now."

She laughs at this, and I realize that she is just as full of conflicts and contradictions as the rest of us. She just has her own way of dealing with them. As I sit trying to record every thought and word, trying to stop the keys on my laptop from expanding and contracting under my fingertips, she sits back calmly, content to admit to her contradictions as if she were outside of herself looking in. Sarah's chosen method of managing her personal paradoxes appears to be by disconnecting from reality just long enough to forget herself entirely. "I feel like no one should interfere with your addiction," she offers, "if it's not interfering with your life."

As the random assertions pile up, I get a sudden and overwhelming impression that this must be what it feels like to be a Catholic priest behind the confessional curtain. Before the image can escape my impaired recollection, Sarah confirms it: "I mean, I definitely identify as Muslim, but I don't follow any of the rules really. I think that people turn religion into rules because they can't think or don't want to. I mean, like, I love sex. I think that when you have an orgasm, that's the closest we can ever get to holiness. I just don't think most people can even entertain that thought without feeling guilty or dirty or shameful. I'm not saying the rules don't matter or make sense. They do. I'm just saying that they shouldn't limit your thoughts or ideas."

Just as Sarah finishes saying this, some three hours into our interview, her girlfriend walks in and asks if the interrogation is going anywhere. Lia is pale, compact, and emaciated. She has a boy's haircut. She is the physical antithesis of Sarah, whose thick mass of tight curly hair atop her head, along with her curvaceous figure, her distinctive sense of style, and her exaggeratedly large eyes, give her the distinct aura and appearance of a neo-African goddess. The two of them could be poster children for the notion "opposites attract." Still, at a quick glance, most people would first take note of one glaring similarity—the fact that they are both women.

While some Muslims choose to interpret the Qur'an and the hadiths as condemning homosexuality or bisexuality as if it were a choice, this is certainly not the only interpretation out there. Heterosexuality is not one of the pillars of Islam, and one's sexual orientation would appear to have little, if any, bearing on one's personal ability to submit to God, which is in fact the definition of Islam. While I doubt that the academic or practical debates about whether homosexuality or bisexuality is "permissible" in Islam will ever reach a consensus, there is at least one consensus established in the Qur'an: "God declares the truth, and He is the best of judges" (6:57). I imagine that there would be far less controversy and intolerance within much of the "Muslim world" if Muslims could just follow the example set forth by the Qur'an, accept that God is the *only* true and ultimate Judge, and withhold their own useless and idle mortal judgments—especially about issues and emotions with which they have no personal experience. On the topic of her sexuality, Sarah has very little to say. She is out to her immediate family, and she's not interested in courting anyone's approval concerning her sexual orientation.

"I find it so tiring how so many of my self-proclaimed Muslim 'brothers' and 'sisters' are so intent on expressing their disapproval of my life or views. It's like they can't stand the possibility that I may not be aware that as far as they're concerned, I'm a bad Muslim. This is why I don't find comfort in the general Muslim community. I wish people could just control the impulse to be constantly sharing their views on religion with you. Religion is a private thing not up for discussion. We can differ in our opinions, but I would never dream of telling a person how she or he *should* practice, so I expect and demand the same kind of respect in return."

I only wish she could get it—if not for her, at least for the rest of us. Turning faith into a normative decree instead of a personal relationship tends to yield painful results. Normative declarations are inherently political—there is nothing introspective or spiritual about them. Sarah's complete refusal to see the world in that light makes her a threat to those who are perpetually trying to cast the shadow of that light anywhere they can to assert power or dominance. Sarah is brimming with love and compassion for all who will accept it, and even some who won't, but she is quick to call things as she sees them. She would be a model whistleblower if the opportunity ever crossed her path, and I hope it has and continues to—again, if not for her, then at least for the rest of us.

Without labeling herself as such, Sarah strikes me as a sincere and dedicated Sufi in many ways. There is definitely something mystical about her, and it has nothing to do with the drugs. Since our interview, Sarah has graduated from Wesleyan, eased off the mind-altering substances, moved to New York, and married a Sudanese filmmaker: a man. She ran this by me with her signature subtlety in an e-mail after months of zero correspondence. I should have known better than to be shocked, but I admit that I was. In between idle banter she wrote:

"I'm based in NYC, but have been blessed with a lot of traveling this year. I got married (to a boy—yes, I'm not joking). He is wonderful!! I'm in a band right now doing Arabic influenced music from the eastern coast of Africa. We will be recording a short demo next week. I'll put it up on my website if you want to see it. Other than that, same old same old: making problems for conservatives worldwide and trying to prove to everyone that it does pay to live for the moment and do whatever I damn well please."

It's typical Sarah to drop something like her marriage in between accounts of her travels and her recent East African–inspired recordings. Again, I should have known better than to be shocked or jarred, but I couldn't help e-mailing her back in utter selfishness and disbelief: "Are you kidding me? You got married? Details! . . . Jesus Christ, you're making this book hard for me. Figures you wouldn't let me squish you into a box and label you."

Damn right, she wouldn't let me squish her into a box. Free spirits can be ruthlessly annoying that way. But true to form, Sarah wrote me back: "I know you can't put me in a box, but this is for your own good so you can be more creative as a writer. Maybe you can even invent a label for me."

Given any leeway, I generally take it, and I'm not about to let this opportunity pass me by. Sarah is unapologetically a lover of as many things and as many people as will permit it. And even permission sometimes becomes irrelevant, as she is just so overtly consumed with this at once frightening and adorable human capacity for love. She provides a "bio" on her Web site that relates few details about her life but provides terrific insight into her soul: "I practice love in all its forms. . . . My god is made of joy, and I worship through love in all its forms."

✦✦✦ ❯❯❯

As I polish off the last Oreo, my vision begins to go fuzzy as my contacts start floating off into the corners of my eyes completely of their own accord. I turn to look at Sarah, whose hair, thanks to my newly impaired sight and the halogen desk lamp on the bedside table, begins to look more and more like a halo floating nearly a foot above her head. I'm not quite sure what happened after that, and the recording provides no clues. The next thing I remember from my first brief encounter with Sarah is waking up the next morning while she was still sleeping and leaving her a note to thank her for being so kind, honest, and welcoming.

After making the bed in Sarah's guest room and placing my note on the nightstand beside it, I peeked into Sarah's room to make sure she hadn't woken up. She was still sound asleep, and I said a short prayer of thanks and blessing as I quietly shut her bedroom door and left. I was headed to Roxana's parents' house, my home base during this weeklong trip that I had made to Connecticut to interview Sarah and Ameer. Driving to see Roxana in my stark white Suzuki hatchback rental car, I felt an overwhelming and unfamiliar mix of joy and empowerment.

I had just met these two incredible people who had both unknowingly reaffirmed my faith in intuition, reason, and divine guidance in every aspect of our lives. Sarah and Ameer, although they lived less than an hour's drive away from one another, were worlds apart in terms of their background and personalities. Still, I knew that if they could meet each other, they would immediately be able to look past their obvious differences and recognize their devoted mutual friends

Sarah

in music and Islam. They wouldn't need me to introduce them to get along. I knew that they were both quick enough to see through exteriors, and if they ever met, I had no doubt that they would get on swimmingly.

Coming to Connecticut to interview Sarah and Ameer was at first a terrifying trip for me. I was a law-school dropout; I was in no way gainfully employed; I was writing a book that lacked a title, a publisher, or an advance; and, three months shy of my twenty-fifth birthday, I was going to have to rent a car in my own name. But during the short scenic drive down the Merritt Parkway from Middletown to Orange to see Roxana, my fears began to subside. I realized that I had managed to do more than rent a car, despite my youth and abysmal driving record. I had also managed to meet two individuals who had inspired me not only to tell their stories but also to tell my own. At a crucial point in my life, Ameer had reminded me that faith was far greater than dogma. And the very next day, through her example, Sarah had shown me just how the beauty of faith could in fact tower over the rigidity of rules. The woman is indeed a force. She's the kind of person you can't forget, not just for her stunning face or her haunting voice but, most of all, for her overwhelming spirit.

SIX

Faisal R.

No vision can grasp Him [God].
But His grasp is over
All vision: He is
Above all comprehension,
Yet is acquainted with all things.

—QUR'AN, AL AN'AM (THE CATTLE), 6:103.

Let the beauty we love be what we do.
There are hundreds of ways to kneel and kiss the ground.

—RUMI, THIRTEENTH-CENTURY
PERSIAN SUFI POET AND MYSTIC

Like many first-generation Americans living in different diasporas, as the children of what our countries of origin consider an unfortunate brain drain and what the U.S. considers prodigious examples of the successful pursuit of the American dream, I have found myself drawn to friends who, like myself, cannot help but live in the past and the future simultaneously: those who share the same uncertainty about their identities in the present instant and the same proud, knowing, and assured conviction about their respective identities in the past. Faisal is one of those friends, and his story stands out.

I met Faisal through Christina, another COFOB—a Coptic Egyptian American, to be precise—whom I met in Mr. Schenk's ninth-grade honors English class and who has been my best friend ever since. Faisal went to school with Christina at NEOUCOM, and he hated it just about as much as she did. For anyone lucky enough to be unfamiliar with the Cleveland and Akron metropolitan areas, NEOUCOM stands for the North Eastern Ohio Universities College of Medicine. It's one of those medical programs that combines college and med school into an inordinately torturous six or seven years. Faisal and Christina both graduated with the class of 2005, and at the time of our interview, Faisal was soon to begin working as an anesthesiology resident at the Cleveland Clinic Foundation, where he continues to work today.

My most vivid memory of Faisal begins in the backseat of his mom's maroon Mercedes on Christina's twenty-first birthday, some six years before our interview. It was around three o'clock in the morning, and we were driving home from an Ohio State party. After being followed for what seemed like an eternity by a cop who refused to run his siren but preferred to silently ride our ass so close I swear I could hear him breathing, we finally parked. Despite the fact that between the two of them, the cop was undoubtedly the one who was driving like a drunkard, he insisted that Faisal was the intoxicated one. It took him hopping on one leg while perfectly reciting the alphabet backward to convince the officer otherwise. To this day, I can't shake the image of him with his shoulder-length dreads, wearing nothing more than a wife-beater and jeans, politely following the cop's inane instructions. He answered to the task as though he were doing something as routine as pulling out his license and registration, which, incidentally, he was never asked to present. Faisal has had his fair share of run-ins with Ohio law enforcement, mostly but not entirely without cause or culpability. That night, however, was definitely a fine example of an unjustifiable run-in, and curious, I asked him why he thought he was so frequently a party to such unfortunate encounters. I remember his response and the expression that accompanied it—laughing but not kidding—to this day: "It's the melanin."

When I first met him, Faisal was a confusing and contradictory hybrid. His superior intellectual aptitude, his penchant for hallucinogens, his faith, and his philosophical existentialist leanings were constantly and concurrently in conflict and concordance. While his internal conflicts persist today, he has apparently learned to embrace them, as he no longer requires the assistance of chemical substances to tolerate life. He freely admits this and has the short hair, professional attire, inordinately large biceps, and matching tattoos to show for it. Faisal and I both share an annoyingly persistent propensity for thought, and as a result, we also share a similar predisposition toward the melancholic side of the emotional spectrum. This mutual proclivity, I think, is why we continue to be friends despite large gaps in communication due to laziness and geography.

✦✦✦ ✦✦✦

Last summer, after nearly a year's lapse in any direct contact, Faisal happened to be driving through Atlanta on his way to Tampa for a radiology rotation, and I told him he had a place to crash so long as he didn't mind answering a couple questions for my book. He made it to Atlanta late on a Friday night, and within what seemed like minutes of getting inside our condo, he had already passed out on the couch midsentence. Matthew and I threw some blankets over him, debated whether or not to do something infantile (draw on his face, cover his lips with olive oil), ultimately decided (thanks largely, if not entirely, to Matthew) that we were too grown up for such shenanigans, and finally went to bed ourselves, leaving Faisal in peace on the couch.

The next morning, I woke up to find him lounging on that same couch with his huge brown eyes glued to ESPN's *SportsCenter*. He didn't even avert his eyes from the television when he said good morning. So when I asked him if he was ready to submit to my interrogation, he looked less than thrilled, but he came around when I told him that he could keep watching the week's meaningless sports highlights so long as the TV stayed on super-low volume. Before I could start, however, his cell phone rang. It was his mom. After an A'salam Alaikum, I love you and I miss you, his mom asked to talk to me, at which point she thanked me for having Faisal in our home and asked if he was behaving. I told her that he was behaving very nicely and that we were happy to have him. After a few more pleasantries, I handed the phone back. As Faisal was talking to her, I noticed the huge, animated, green and yellow Statue of Liberty sticker on his phone that read, "Hurray! It's summer." When he got off the phone, he told me that he had picked it up during a pediatrics rotation and demanded, to no avail, that I stop making fun of him. I told him to behave and answer my questions or that I would have to call his mom back and tell on him. Being the easygoing kid he is, Faisal ignored my threat, put down his phone, turned up the volume a notch on the TV, and calmly submitted to my inquisition.

Faisal's responses to my questions were so direct, honest, and flat-out hilarious that there is no way that I could tell his story myself any better than he did in his own interview. So at the risk of revealing my own pathetically elementary skills as an interviewer, I have chosen to let him speak for himself here.

Melody: Give me some background: basic criminal profile—age, nationality, family, friends, blood type, Social Security number—go.

Faisal: Um, OK. Twenty-five, born in Queens. I got two parents who are Pakistani. My dad grew up in Karachi his whole life, and he came from a really wealthy family by Pakistani standards—like, my cousins drive Benzes and shit, which is like ridiculous Pakistani-wise. And my mom came from an entirely opposite background.

Melody: Oh, how sweet—it sounds just like a Bollywood movie. Was there lots of dancing and hiding behind trees and fountains?

Faisal: Yeah, mine is bad. My dad was pretty much like, "Hey, she looks good. Get us married." Basically, that's what happened.

Melody: Brothers or sisters?

Faisal: Only spoiled child.

Melody: OK, enough background. Now explain what brought you to America and what being American means to you.

Faisal: I was brought to America by being born here, and so I know no other way to be. When you're immersed in one thing, that's what you choose. When I think of football, I think of an oblong ball and not a spherical one. I know who Carson Daly is, and I wish I didn't—things from my music choice down to my choice in TV shows. I choose to stick to channels I know my cousins from Pakistan would skip. I picture myself growing old in this country as opposed to other countries. I wear my baseball caps backwards. I guess it's just a feeling I have.

Melody: Well put. So now tell me what brought you to Islam, how you practice, why you consider yourself Muslim, that kind of stuff.

Faisal: I was brought to Islam because my parents are both Muslim. The level of their practice was minimal until they got older. Neither one was really religious. My mom started becoming religious after I left for college. She actually went on Hajj, and now she prays five times a day. My dad still doesn't. They sent me to Sunday school at the Islamic Center in Columbus when I was a kid. We would memorize *surahs* and stuff like that. I didn't dislike it—as long as I didn't miss the first quarter of a Browns game I was fine. I considered it like a class, so I excelled, and that's why I think I liked it. I consider myself Muslim because that is how I was taught; that is what I was taught of the divine. I fully believe that any weaknesses in myself can be fixed by Allah. . . .

For a long period, though, I chose not to think about God because I had other priorities—I was more into having fun, I guess. There is a reason people start going toward religion as they get older. I was pretty far away from Islam in my late teens, and it was more a source of guilt. Now I see it as a net to crash on that is still there despite my having neglected it. It's how I've been taught, that's the way I know how to pray—I don't at all believe it is the only way to pray, but it works for me. There is something beautiful about the cohesiveness of a group of people praying in a mosque. To be a part of that is really comforting for me. The fact that there is a huge community out there that will accept me based on nothing else—not on how much money I have or on the way I look or dress or on my skin color or nationality. Solidarity and community is what Islam means to me. I see it as a bridge between cultures that otherwise wouldn't communicate—for the one moment you're praying together, you don't think of anything else but what really matters. I can see a real difference in myself and others between the moments that precede the prayer and those that come after it.

Melody: So, where are you in terms of practicing today? I mean, what stands out as most important to you when it comes to practice?

Faisal: Well, obviously the five pillars. I'm trying to improve my practice, but it isn't easy. I don't pray nearly as much as I wish I did. I pray maybe two times a week. In terms of Ramadan, I have fasted and not fasted, and when I don't fast I feel bad for not fasting and when I do fast I feel better. *Zakat*, though, is my favorite pillar—even though it's a pretty small percentage that we're required to give, I think charity is really important and should be integral in all religions.

I haven't been to Mecca for Hajj yet, but I have been there on Umrah [Umrah is often referred to as a mini-pilgrimage, but unlike Hajj, it is not a requirement but simply a great blessing, which can be performed any time during the year]. There were so many people, and I was shocked by the fact that there was so much crazy money all over the place. Merchants would leave Rolexes and diamonds out there where anyone could easily steal them—but no one would dare.

Seeing the Kaaba was cool—somewhat surreal. It gave me chills every time I looked at it. I just wish that sensation could have lasted longer. One night, I helped this blind guy walk around the Kaaba. He was talking to me, and I had no idea what he was saying because he was speaking a language I couldn't even guess at. I felt so lucky to be able to help him. What I really liked was that all these people were walking around and having their own private conversations with God, and we were all dressed the same and the men and the women were mixed, so you couldn't see any difference between a CEO and a goat farmer. Before going there, the largest crowd I had ever been a part of was at the new OSU football stadium. I imagine there were at least a million people—all praying in unison. I've just never seen more people in one place—people everywhere, and five times a day in that city everyone drops everything and prays. People are super-emotional, and you can imagine they would be, so many of them having saved their entire lives just to make that one trip. It's surreal even to think about it.

Melody: What, if anything, concerns you about the way non-Muslim Americans view Islam? If you could change one thing about that perception, what would it be?

Faisal: They *don't* view Islam. They don't look at more than a five-second news clip. They see Islam as a threat. They don't ever bother to learn about it. They don't know that "Islam" means submission to God. And I don't say universally, and I also don't blame people because they are overwhelmed by media and images that are negative. If I could change one thing, I would want people here to realize that there are almost always like fifteen sides to every story. I would want them to not be so quick to judge—it has just become such a Pavlovian response in this country: if terrorism, then Islam. Calling Islam the cause of crazy shit like that, without even mentioning American foreign policy, is a cop-out response. There are plenty of Muslims who aren't like that, and there are plenty of people who aren't Muslim who hate the U.S.

Melody: What, if anything, concerns you about your own community's take on Islam, and if you could change one thing about *that* perception what would it be?

Faisal: In Pakistan, a lot of people are uneducated about Islam—a lot don't know how to read, and even the ones who do often just rather rely on what other people say. Basically, most people just don't do the bookwork. It's a pretty ridiculous misconception that if you have a really big beard you obviously know what you're talking about. If I could change something there, I would make people start reading for themselves and stop listening to imams instead of their own reason.

Melody: What are some of the most memorable reactions you've experienced from others upon discovering that you are Muslim?

Faisal: People have tried to convert me to Christianity multiple times. At one point, one of my closest friends, Kevin, was really serious about trying to convert me. He was doing it in a nice way, though, so I wasn't offended because he just wanted me to be saved, and he really thought I was going to hell and genuinely wanted me to go to heaven. Yeah, it didn't work, though [laughing].

One of my surgery attendings during this last rotation said flat-out that he just didn't like Muslims the first time I met him—he said he didn't know any Muslims, but he just didn't like them. I think your religion is a private thing, and since I really wasn't feelin' this guy, I wasn't about to fill him in. Also, I just didn't feel like getting into it, especially with someone who could make my life a living hell for the next two months if he wanted to.

Melody: Did he really just say, "I don't like Muslims"? Why didn't you rail on him?

Faisal: His exact statement was "I'm very fearful of these Muslims."

Melody: Fucking moron! Seriously, why didn't you kick his ass right there on the operating table—I mean after you were sure that the surgery had gone fine and all [laughing]?

Faisal: Honestly, these guys are grading me. You have to kiss their ass. I don't kiss their ass at all like most of the kids, but I'm not going to try to give them a reason to screw me over—no matter how stupid it may seem. The same guy did say something to my friend Charlie, though. Charlie's a convert, and he's also in the U.S. Army, so he reported him, I think. I don't make an effort to let people know that I'm Muslim. Whereas a lot of people spoke up after 9–11, I didn't go out of my way to speak up afterwards. Maybe that passivity is hiding it in a way, but it just takes so much to educate a happily ignorant person—I'd rather not.

I remember this track meet in sixth grade. I was hanging with my friends—JJ and Desmond—I think we were warming up for the meet or something, and we overheard this hilljack kid say, "Well that there's a nigger, an oriental, and I don't know what the hell *that* one is." I guess I'm used to people not knowing what the hell I am, and I don't see how telling them is going to change them in any way—other than giving them jargon to work with. I don't feel like I can change people like that. I feel like maybe I'll just absorb some of their negativity, so that overall there would be less.

Melody: Um, OK. I think that's crap, but let's move on.

Faisal: Fine, screw you. Your feet smell.

Melody: Whatever—can we continue?

Faisal: Fine.

Melody: OK, September 11th. Where were you, what were you doing, and any thoughts?

Faisal: I was studying liver pathology at the time—skipping class and reading. I got a call from Desmond.

Melody: The same kid from the track meet?

Faisal: Yeah. Anyway, he's in the Navy now, and he was stationed in South Carolina at the time—he's in South Korea now. So, he called me when only one of the towers had fallen—he told me to go turn on the TV. I remember thinking, "God, I hope this is just some crazy white guy," but other than that I was just in shock like everybody else. I remember being really sad when I saw people jumping out of windows. It was crazy. I just felt really sad.

Melody: What are your hopes and expectations for your children?

Faisal: Um, great segue, Mom. I don't even have a girlfriend.

Melody: Whatever, I'm getting sick and tired of this garbage. You're really not as interesting as I thought you would be [laughing]. Really, you're boring as hell.

Faisal: Die.

Melody: OK, I promise. After you answer this one last question.

Faisal: Fine, if you promise. What was the question again?

Melody: Your hypothetical kids! What do you expect from them? [Since our interview, Faisal has gotten engaged to a Muslim Indian American physician. When we last spoke, he was very excited about getting married, and he mentioned their mutual intention to have three children.]

Faisal: My expectation is that they are hardworking and not lazy—that the lazy gene skips a generation. I'm going to introduce them to every religion and spend time discovering and learning with them. Of course, part of me would love for them to choose Islam, but all I would do to encourage that would be to lead by my own improved example, hopefully. So long as they are well educated and do the research for themselves, they can pick whatever religion they want. I mean, they will definitely be American—but it's their decision whether they are Muslim or not. Generally, if you force anything down someone else's throat, they don't like the way it tastes.

SEVEN

Sanida

On no soul doth God
Place a burden greater
Than it can bear.
It gets every good that it earns,
And it suffers every ill that it
earns.
(Pray:) "Our Lord!
Condemn us not
If we forget or fall
Into error; our Lord!
Lay not on us a burden
Like that which Thou
Didst lay on those before us;
Our Lord! lay not on us
A burden greater than we
Have strength to bear.
Blot out our sins,
And grant us forgiveness.
Have mercy on us.
Thou art our Protector;
Help us against those
Who stand against Faith."

—QUR'AN, AL BAQARAH (THE COW), 2:286

All sects are different because they come from men;
Morality is everywhere the same because it comes from God.

—VOLTAIRE

I noticed Sanida straightaway on the first day of orientation. We were both first-year law students and shared an apparent similar wish to avoid introducing ourselves to strangers over bitter coffee served in blindingly white Styrofoam cups. After surveying the entire class, I had come to the swift conclusion that she, with her bright blue eyes and her impressive collection of tight blond curls, was definitely the prettiest girl in the class. As a result, I already secretly hated her before I even knew her name. We shared all the same classes that year, though, as we were both in "Section F"—a designation that proved ironic in Sanida's case, given her grades, and considerably less so in my case, given mine. After a few weeks in Section F, I noticed that Sanida had a slight accent that I couldn't quite place. One day before Contracts class, I took the liberty of asking her where she was from, and she promptly informed me that she was Bosnian. I knew enough about the former Yugoslavia to make the connection between Bosnian and Muslim, but I still couldn't believe that this blondie could be Muslim.

"But you're not *Muslim?*" I blurted.

"Yes I am," she responded. "Sanida is a Muslim name. Why? *You're* not Muslim."

"Uh, yeah," I responded. "What—the brown skin, eyes, and hair didn't clue you in?"

"Well, your name *is* Melody," she retorted. "What kind of Muslim name is that?"

For the first time, I smiled at her—taking comfort in the fact that I wasn't the only one fooled by appearances. We both laughed at our mutual ignorance, and within a couple of weeks, we were inseparable. I once overheard one of our classmates refer to us as a set of matching Chia Pets. Considering the fact that we both have an abundance of hair, and that we had taken to sitting next to each other toward the front of every class, the analogy was fair. From behind, apparently, we looked like two bobbing heads with way too much hair. I was forever being asked where my "partner in crime" was whenever I dared traverse the law school without her. We were indeed a team, and though I know that she could and would have easily done it without me, I have sincere doubts as to whether I would have made it through that first year without her. I have genuinely loathed very few things more than law school, especially the first year, but Sanida made the whole thing bearable for me. And when I dropped out for a semester to finish this book, it was Sanida who convinced me, more than anyone else, to come back.

Sanida grew up in a small town in northern Herzegovina called Jablanica. Her father, Muhamed, was a successful businessman in Herzegovina before the war, and he was always traveling to Slovenia, Austria, and Germany for business. He ran a company that contracted with granite mines and engraved tombstones and plaques with various gold and silver impressions. One of the most popular orders, apparently, was for a block of granite engraved with Tito's image, entirely in gold. Sanida says that she had three such blocks in her house at one point. Her mother, Sabina, is a teacher who instructs middle-school students in chemistry and biology. Sanida attributes her strong appreciation for the value of education to her mother's influence, and I have no doubt that this influence has considerably shaped the person she is today.

Sanida was fourteen years old when the war broke out in May 1992. When I ask her when the war reached her town, she tells me the exact date and time: one o'clock P.M. on April 15, 1993. She was sitting in her living room with a cousin who had just come to live with her family after fighting in the Bosnian Army and eventually escaping northern Bosnia. She heard an explosion and assumed it was just some drunk soldier outside of a bar setting off a bomb for fun (apparently a fairly common occurrence, she tells me, where generally no one got hurt). Her cousin, however, having fought in the war, recognized the sound immediately as a shell and told her to go to the basement while he went outside to see where it was coming from. She ignored his orders and followed him outside, just in time to see the shell whiz overhead and hit a factory less than half a mile away. Five more shells exploded that day, and it would be two long years before the shelling stopped.

During those two years, Sanida finished high school and learned English by reading books during the sleepless nights she spent with her family in the basement of their home, waiting for the shelling to stop. She wanted to work as an interpreter for the United Nations during the war, but she was told that she could not begin working until she had graduated from high school. By the time she finished school, however, the war was officially over, but interpreters were still needed to help train the Bosnian police forces in keeping peace and quelling ethnic tensions. She started working for the U.N. directly after her high-school graduation. She laughs now, explaining how the U.N. sent Nigerian, Pakistani, and Indian police to teach the new Bosnian force to respect human rights and refuse bribes. Considering that Nigeria, Pakistan, and India all have serious problems with corruption and human rights violations within their own governments and police forces, it's little wonder that the training sessions were minimally effective.

✳✳✳ ✳✳✳

Sanida too is a writer, and as we sit on my balcony, some twenty stories up, she tells me not to write too much because one day she wants to write her own story. I laugh, knowing that she could fill fifteen novels, let alone one dazzling memoir, full of hilarious and heartbreaking prose, given her talent, her experience, and her incredibly distinct voice and perspective. I assure her that there will still be plenty left to tell, and reassured, she starts talking about Ihsan.

Ihsan, Sanida's Turkish commander, spoke very little English. One evening, upon receiving a call from an American officer in the neighboring city of Mostar, Ihsan understood that there was a party going on there and that he and his colleagues (Sanida and two Pakistani officers) were invited. Upon arriving in Mostar, however, Sanida quickly realized that there was indeed no party. Quite to the contrary, there was a massacre in the works. A group of Muslims had come to the Croatian side of the city to visit the graves of their loved ones, and the Croats were throwing stones at them. At the center of the conflict stood nearly forty Spanish NATO soldiers, smoking cigarettes and watching, their weapons at their sides. Some of the Croats were even shooting machine guns at the crowd of mourners, while the NATO soldiers, whose job it was to prevent such incidents, just stood idly by in some sort of catatonic daze.

Sanida could do little more than report the incident, but as her commander Ihsan drove their U.N. jeep away from the center of the conflict, they soon approached a group of Bosnians beating a Croatian man who just happened to be driving through the area. Sanida recognized that the man was a Croat from his license plate and immediately told Ihsan to drive forward, convinced that once the Bosnians saw the U.N. jeep they would stop. Ihsan refused, and Sanida ran out of the car toward the men, Ihsan running after her. The sight of Ihsan running after Sanida in his U.N. uniform apparently sufficed to scare off the Bosnians, who were more than likely seeking revenge on an innocent man for what was happening to their own people some five miles away. The Croatian man immediately leaped back into his car and sped off before Sanida could make sure that he was OK.

This is how most of Sanida's war stories end. There are few resolutions and even fewer explanations. I cannot imagine having seen such atrocities, and then having to witness such incredibly anticlimactic conclusions, such cowardice and such pathetically inadequate resolutions.

Sanida admits that by the time of the massacre in Mostar, she was beginning to become disenchanted with her ability help her country and her people by working for the U.N. She had apparently always wanted to come to the United States. Long before the war, when Sanida was still a child, her father had promised that he would send her to San Francisco to study journalism. After the war, however, her family, once one of the wealthiest in all of Herzegovina, was broke. They had lost nearly all of their money in banks that collapsed. Nevertheless, Sanida was determined to fulfill her and her father's plan for her, even if it meant that she would be coming to America as a refugee. With the assistance of Velma, a distant cousin already in America who agreed to sponsor her through the International Rescue Committee, her dream became possible. Sanida is exceedingly grateful to Velma, and even now, five years later, she talks about her as if she were a saint or a seraph, and not a living person who resides only a couple miles from where we sit.

When Sanida first left Bosnia to come to America, she told her mom before she left that if she caught her crying at all she'd refuse to leave, and somehow, despite witnessing the sadness and tears of everyone around her, Sanida's mother managed to suppress her emotions for the sake of her only daughter. Sanida didn't see her mother shed a single tear during that time. Her father, Muhamed, also played stoic for his daughter until the very last moment. Driving away, however, Sanida turned to witness her father, a sizeable man of nearly fifty years, collapse onto the ground and start weeping uncontrollably. She tells me this, and the second she notices my eyes filling with tears, she scolds me: "Don't you start crying. I swear. If you start crying, this interview is over. Don't do it!" I control myself, and she continues telling me how happy she was when she finally got to the U.S. and how she knew that all of her sacrifices would be worthwhile.

Sanida did not come to the U.S. alone. She came as part of a group of forty refugees from all over the former Yugoslavia. After two separate eight-hour bus rides, from Jablanica to Zagreb and from Zagreb to Vienna, they took a plane from Vienna to New York. She remembers a seventeen-year-old Bosnian boy from Sandzak, Serbia, whose only belongings fit in a Ziploc freezer bag—three pairs of socks, a toothbrush, and an audiotape of folk music; she remembers being the only one who spoke English and, therefore, the group's unofficial tour guide; she remembers the Austrians gawking at them as if they were animals in a zoo; she remembers the shock of those in the group who had never left their small villages at seeing a bustling city airport; she remembers being told over and over again not to lose their IOM (Internal Organization for Migration) bags, which held all the documents that would allow them to enter the U.S. as refugees, without passports or Green Cards; she remembers the sheer humiliation, exhaustion, and sadness that characterized that journey; and she remembers that the first kind official they encountered on this trip, the first who looked them in the eyes and smiled at them, was an American immigration officer at JFK, welcoming them all to the United States and telling them, "The U.S. welcomes you, hosts you, and you are refugees. Hold onto your IOM bags." Today, Sanida no longer has her IOM bag. She now has an American passport, and she is just as quick to tell you that she is American as she is to tell you that she is Bosnian. Still, she didn't become an American overnight.

When Sanida first arrived in Atlanta, only days after her arrival in New York City, she reported to the International Rescue Committee (IRC), as it was the organization handling her resettlement program, which would find her a job and an apartment and provide her with three months' rent and food stamps. Sanida was determined to integrate and assimilate into American culture, and she knew that if she left her housing decision up to the IRC, she'd likely end up with other Bosnians. Accordingly, she found herself an apartment within walking distance of her work, less than a month after coming to Atlanta. Because her English was so advanced, she was given a job working as a receptionist at the front desk of the Grand Hyatt Hotel in Buckhead. She worked there for one year, perfecting her English and, among other things, checking in George Hamilton, Whitney Houston, and Allen Iverson.

Apparently, the Hyatt had made as much of a habit out of hiring immigrants and refugees as it had out of accommodating celebrities. Sanida occasionally worked reception with a Korean girl named Sook, and one night, when they were changing shifts, Sanida was in the middle of telling Puff Daddy that they had no rooms available. He was apparently growing increasingly livid as Sanida was growing increasingly exhausted, so she handed him over to Sook, telling him that her shift had just ended and that Sook would be happy to tend to him.

Neither Sanida nor Sook had any idea who the hell Puff Daddy was, and even if they had, I'm pretty sure that they wouldn't have cared. Recognizing his anonymity among the largely FOB staff, however, Puffy finally pulled the number-one disgustingly pretentious celebrity stunt: "Do you *know* who I *am?*" Sook admitted that she hadn't a clue, and as Sanida was getting her stuff together to go home, she overheard this. Sook was evidently of quite minimal stature and girth, and she also had a reputation for being calm, quiet, and collected. But when Puff Daddy informed her who he was, and when of course she still didn't know what that meant, Sook leaned across the front desk and unabashedly replied: "Well, I'm Puff *Sook*, and I don't care!" This was enough to throw Puffy and his whole entourage into a huge fit of laughter, and he ultimately backed off until a room soon became magically available.

The year Sanida spent working at the Hyatt thus gave her an education in American pop culture, American society, and a wide variety of American immigrant cultures and subcultures. In Bosnia, before the war, she was the child of wealthy and prominent parents—a genuinely spoiled brat in her own right. But in the U.S., it was a much different story—she was a straight-up FOB, and accordingly, she was in for all the struggles and setbacks that so commonly characterize that experience. But Sanida, unlike many of her Bosnian friends in Atlanta, lived up to the expectations and dreams she had for herself.

While she was working at the Hyatt, she made no secret of the fact that she intended to become a lawyer one day. One of her Bosnian coworkers evidently used to laugh at this, saying that she was too pretty—that she would just marry a rich guy, and that would be that. After graduating from law school, Sanida went back to the Hyatt and found this particular former coworker still working there. Upon learning that she had in fact followed through with her plans, and that she had no husband supporting her, he was visibly shocked. Indeed, it would have been easy for Sanida to just marry rich and become an unemployed socialite, but she had other plans for herself, and they didn't involve codependency any more than they involved checking in pompous Puff Daddies for the rest of her life.

That year, while she was working at the Hyatt, Sanida was accepted to Agnes Scott College in Atlanta. At Agnes Scott, she double majored in French and international relations, with a focus on transnational identity. By the time she graduated in 2002, with a nearly flawless academic record, she had already been accepted to Emory Law School.

Although her father passed away unexpectedly just days before Sanida started her first year of law school, he did see her finish college and knew that she would make a success of herself in America. After the war, Sanida says, he used to always tell everyone that one day his daughter would prosecute

Milosevic at The Hague. After having finished her first year of law school with notable academic success, Sanida spent a summer working for a nonprofit social services organization that provided legal assistance to immigrants and refugees. The next year, she continued her academic success and won the prize for "Best Oralist" in the law school's moot court competition. Although I took great amusement in the word choice for that award, as did many of our classmates, we all agreed with her selection, knowing that we dreaded the day that we would ever have to stand as her opposing counsel.

Sanida has a remarkably strong sense of justice, not to mention a sharp tongue and lightning-fast reflexes. Despite the fact that, given her grades, Sanida could have worked at any number of high-paying corporate law firms, she chose to take a position as a prosecutor with the New York City Law Department, Family Court Division. While Milosevic may have escaped her grasp in death, she still aspires to one day prosecute his allies around the world. I wouldn't be surprised to see her eventually prosecuting war criminals within the Sudanese Janjaweed or the Ugandan Lord's Resistance Army. Sanida will no doubt continue to prove her father proud, even from this distance.

⁄⁄⁄ ⟫⟫⟫

Sanida is the epitome of a "tough cookie." I have seen her cry a total of two times, and I have never seen anyone single-handedly win more arguments. She is a master of persuasion and rational argument, in many ways a one-woman show, and if I could predict her timing with any accuracy, I swear I'd find a way to sell tickets. After our first year of law school, I decided to pursue a joint degree, which included a master's in public health. Thus, I spent much of my second year at Emory's School of Public Health, and Sanida often picked me up after my classes there. I had come to expect that she would be late—Bosnian time, she called it. Since I have known her, Sanida has persistently and notoriously used her status as a "Bosnian refugee" as an excuse for anything and everything— tardiness, brashness, countless varieties of foolishness, you name it.

As she pulled up one day, nearly thirty minutes late, Sanida parked her car illegally and stepped out. I knew what she was up to. She was an ardent smoker back then, and I think she took a distinct pleasure in smoking in front of the School of Public Health, which by the way was also attached to the Nursing School. I admit that I sort of appreciated the irony as well, but I also appreciated the carcinogenic consequences of smoking.

On this particular smoke break, a student in scrubs approached us on her

Sanida

way into the Nursing School and began literally scolding Sanida: "I can't believe you're doing that here of all places! Don't you know it can *kill* you!" Not so incidentally, this student was roughly one hundred pounds overweight. Being the proud and brazen Bosniak that she is, Sanida calmly told the woman that if she was so concerned with public health, then maybe she should start by getting off her lazy ass and engaging in some gravely needed aerobic exercise. This shut up the nursing student pretty quickly, and she proceeded to leave us in peace, still sporting the same expression of shock and disgust that she had worn when she first approached us.

Since then, Sanida has quit smoking, but woe to anyone who tries to scold her for anything. She's the kind of person who will be defiant out of spite alone if she finds it appropriate, just to remind you that nobody is the boss of her. But, lucky for her and even luckier for the rest of us, she is only very rarely wrong. It's hard to tell for sure, though, given the fact that the girl is just so damn persuasive. Granted the will and the opportunity, she could convince a gay black pro-choice environmentalist to vote Republican. Thank God, however, she has chosen to use her powers for good. She'd be a hell of a liability otherwise.

✿✿✿ ✦✦✦

When I ask Sanida why she considers herself American as well as Bosnian, she says that, despite being more jaded today about the possibilities this country represents, she still believes that if she works hard enough she can make something of herself and that she will not be held back in life because of her race, religion, or ethnicity. "When I go back to Bosnia," she explains, "I get irritated by the prejudices I see even within my own community, a kind of prejudice that I remember but that never used to bother me until I came here. America has turned me into a much more open-minded and tolerant person. I have learned to accept homosexuals and people of different races, and I know that this part of me that accepts those who are presumably so different than me is very American."

She cannot forget that in Bosnia, there were people trying to kill her because she was Muslim, people who tried to say that she and her people didn't exist, that they were all just failures of Tito's Yugoslavian experiment who were really just Serbian or Croatian. Sanida didn't find out that she was Muslim until the war began. In her house, there were copies of the Qur'an, the Talmud, and the Bible. "We were international," she explains. "I didn't believe in God until I was fourteen, when they attacked us. Before that, Tito was the closest thing I knew to God."

While she may not have fully understood what it meant to be Muslim while she was growing up, her family still celebrated Muslim holidays, and her parents both knew and recited many *surahs* from the Qur'an by heart. Indeed, she grew up in a Muslim household and engaged in distinctly "Muslim" activities; she simply failed to make the association between religion and faith until the beginning of the war. Her best friend, Gabriella, was Croatian, and up until the war broke out, Sanida never fully understood why her family, unlike Gabriella's, never put up a Christmas tree until after Christmas, or why when she knocked on doors for eggs at Easter, her Muslim neighbors laughed, while telling her that they had no eggs. Later, she would learn that Christmas and Easter are Christian holidays; she would learn that her family only put up a Christmas tree to celebrate the new year; she would learn that Muslims don't celebrate Easter; she would learn to tell the difference between Christian and Muslim names; and she would learn that these differences mattered immeasurably to many of those around her.

Gabriella stayed in Bosnia, graduated from high school, and recently married. Sanida explains that Gabriella came from a good, honest Catholic family and that they suffered a lot. Gabriella's dad was taken prisoner during the war by Bosnians who insisted that he was a spy, despite the fact that he was an ailing sixty-year-old man who couldn't even read.

Sanida has since lost contact with Gabriella. "I think my life here would shock her," Sanida explains. "I think she would think I was too Americanized, and I know she'd be right. The two of us are just really different now." Still, Sanida makes a point of adding that Gabriella "really is a good honest Catholic girl" and that her brothers, who were supposed to be fighting on the front lines of the Croatian army against the Bosnians, refused to fight. "We didn't find out until later," she tells me, "that they didn't fight. Her family really went through a lot, and they didn't deserve any of it. None of us did."

Sanida recounts that only a few weeks after hearing the news of the bravery of Gabriella's Christian brothers, she witnessed some of the most unfathomable cowardice that she has ever or since experienced from her own supposedly "Muslim brothers." After the war, some of the Saudi Arabian soldiers who had come to fight in the Bosnian Army stayed in Jablanica. These *mujahideen* soldiers were insistent that the Bosnian Muslims in Sanida's hometown were not practicing Islam properly. They shot at young girls swimming in a lake because they were dressed "immodestly" in swimsuits, and as their final farewell, they beat up two teenagers whom they found making out in a car in the hills one night. After the latter incident, according to Sanida, all of the Bosnians in Jablanica joined together to kick out the Saudis, making it clear that their twisted version of Islam was unacceptable in Jablanica. Unjustified aggression is just as great a sin in Islam as it is in most other religions—clearly, it is an offense far greater than kissing or swimming could ever be—but unfortunately, some Muslims find themselves so caught up in the appearance and "modesty" of others that they overlook even the most basic teachings of Islam.

Sanida is proud that her town was able to rid itself of this parasitic mockery of Islam, and she hopes that the rest of the world will be able to do the same. "Muslims need to be more tolerant of each other," she maintains. "Just because someone prays five times a day and dresses modestly, it doesn't automatically mean she's a good person, and just because someone doesn't pray or dress appropriately, it doesn't automatically make her a horrible person." Sanida explains that the imam in Jablanica was a prolific thief and thug—always with his hands in some sort of murky business deal. She insists that no one had any respect for him. Indeed, those who are most intent on imposing perceived religious doctrines and restrictions on others are often themselves the most lacking in moral fortitude.

Unfortunately, this small-town Bosnian mullah presents an example of a phenomenon that is not isolated to the practice—or, more appropriately stated, the malpractice—of Islam. Religious officials guilty of severe malpractice can be found within all of the world's religions. Nevertheless, Muslims in particular have recently suffered enormous injury as a result of the words and actions of our supposed leaders, those who claim to be acting in the name of God when they are truly acting only in the name of power and lunacy at best.

Sanida is not particularly religious. She is not highly concerned with public perceptions and misperceptions about her faith. She doesn't claim to be fulfilling God's lofty plans for her, she doesn't aspire to martyrdom, and she certainly doesn't hold herself higher than anyone else simply because she is Muslim or because she has suffered because of her allegiance to her faith and heritage. Yet she is uncompromisingly Muslim and American, and she blames neither Muslims nor Americans for telling her that being both is impossible. She knows better herself, and as far as she's concerned, "impossible" has always been both a challenge and a compliment.

EIGHT

Molham

Behold! In the creation
Of the heavens and the earth;
In the alternation
Of the Night and the Day;
In the sailing of the ships
Through the Ocean
For the profit of mankind;
In the rain which God
Sends down from the skies,
And the life which He gives therewith
To an earth that is dead;
In the beasts of all kinds
That He scatters
Through the earth;
In the change of the winds,
And the clouds which they
Trail like their slaves
Between the sky and the earth—
(Here) indeed are Signs
For a people who are wise.

—QUR'AN, AL BAQARAH (THE COW), 2:164

I do not feel obliged to believe that the same God
who has endowed us with sense, reason, and intellect has
intended us to forgo their use.

—GALILEO GALILEI, "LETTER TO THE
GRAND DUCHESS CHRISTINA" (1615)

When Molham suggested the Four Seasons as our first meeting place, I thought he was either trying to impress me with his sophisticated taste or test me to see if stuff like that carried any weight in my eyes. I had no idea that he had offices there, let alone that he lived there. I mean, who, other than spoiled heiresses and rock stars, actually *lives* in the Four Seasons? Molham does. But he definitely didn't grow up there.

As a Palestinian born in 1969, Molham grew up all over the place: Beirut, Geneva, Cairo, Athens. He came to the United States in 1984, when he was in the tenth grade, and became a U.S. citizen shortly thereafter. His father was one of eleven children. At around age fifteen, he left his home, a small West Bank village by the name of Burqua, to study agriculture at a vocational school. He taught himself enough to receive a full scholarship to the American University of Beirut and then received an assistantship allowing him to study for his Ph.D. at Auburn University in Alabama. After finishing his Ph.D., Molham's father accepted a job offer from Dupont to work in their agricultural chemicals division. After a few months of training in Delaware, he was sent to Lebanon, where he met Molham's mom.

The youngest of thirteen children, she had spent most of her youth in a Catholic boarding school in Beirut. When she was nine, her mother died in a car accident in Lebanon, just after her family moved there from Senegal, where they had owned and run a profitable textile company. After her mother's death, she remained in boarding school, her older sister taking on the role of her guardian until she turned nineteen, when she met Molham's father, who was eight years her senior. After a six-month courtship, they married, and less than a year later, Molham was born in Beirut.

Molham describes his mother as artistic and refined: "She was into ballet, art, music. You know, that kind of stuff." His tone changes entirely when he describes his father: "He's a work-hard, school-school-school, rainy-day, disaster-scenario kind of guy." This "rainy-day, disaster" mentality, however, has proven useful, given his father's experiences, and may in fact have been a result of some of those experiences. After the Six Day War, while he was still studying at Auburn, Molham's dad immediately became a refugee, unwelcome in his own homeland. He couldn't go back to live with his mom or his sister because all Palestinians who were outside of the country during the war were prohibited by the new Israeli government from reentering as anything more than tourists.

"None of us have any rights there. We can at least visit now, but today someone who lives in Russia who happens to be Jewish has more rights there than any of us do. I went back in 2000, after twenty-seven years, when my sister, Lana, graduated from MIT. Her present to herself was a trip back. We went together for three weeks. We visited Jordan, the West Bank, and Lebanon. We saw our cousins and aunts, who we hadn't seen in forever, but it wasn't all tea and roses. They were all still confined to their homes and they continue to be, with tanks outside their front doors to constantly remind them that they are unwelcome in their own land. It's a kind of neo–separate but equal policy they have toward us. [Noam] Chomsky said that the ultimate insult to the memory of the people who lost their lives in the Holocaust is to adopt the central doctrine of their oppressors. He's right. It's crazy how the concept of a Jewish nation is somehow not offensive, how it's somehow considered a noble achievement and can still be called a democracy, whereas any other form of theocracy is readily seen as inherently unfair and undemocratic. To me this isn't a Jew versus Muslim thing. . . . This is about a Zionist movement, widely discredited by the Jewish community until World War II. Before that, it was just a fringe right-wing political movement. Really, this whole thing could be resolved overnight, though."

"What?!" I blurt, nearly spitting my Diet Coke out in his face. "Are you talking about the whole Israeli-Palestinian conflict? You've got to be kidding me."

"No, not kidding. Really, it could all end tomorrow if they could just agree to make it a secular state—if we just call a truce long enough to see straight, I think most everyone there would figure out that the only right thing to do is to make it a secular democracy, leaving religion out of it entirely."

"Fine. So what do you call it then?"

"I don't care what you call it. Call it Fred. Whatever you call it, we would all benefit that way. All the energy that both sides are directing toward hate and violence can be redirected toward something constructive for once, even just toward coming up with a new name we can all agree on. It would be the quickest and easiest way to put an end to apartheid there—it didn't work in South Africa, and it's not going to work for us either. Call it what you want, but I don't see a distinction between state terror and individual terror—all I do see is how one feeds off of the other. I mean, like September 11th. What the hell was the idea behind that? Supposedly to get back at America for years of ridiculously oppressive and colonial foreign policies toward Muslims and the Middle East. So, when you get down to it, it was supposed to make things easier for those of us from that part of the world. Thing is, though, it certainly hasn't made my life any easier, and I'm pretty sure that most Muslims here and around the world would agree on that."

At the very least, the ones I talked to would agree. There was a consistent concern among many of the young Muslim Americans with whom I spoke in researching and writing this book about fictitious distinctions between state terror (most specifically that of the U.S. and the countries it supports financially and politically) and the criminal terrorist acts committed by individuals representing either themselves or violent extremist groups. While there was an obvious and undeniable overall consensus that the terrorist attacks of September 11, 2001, were unforgivable, heinous, and criminal, there was an equally strong consensus that wearing a suit or a uniform (whether that of a soldier in the Israeli Defense Force or that of a head of state) doesn't mean that someone is somehow magically incapable of criminal or unethical behavior. Suits and uniforms are highly overrated, and considering the acts of many people who choose to don them, there is absolutely no reason to use them as any sort of legal or moral indicator.

All but one of the many Muslim Americans I approached or interviewed for this book gave me a consistent two-pronged response to the subject of terrorism and September 11. First, there was the general statement of disgust and embarrassment at the events and at the fact that the lunatics responsible for them had claimed Islam as their inspiration. Second, there was the qualified addendum: although there is no legitimate justification for killing innocent civilians, it should not be forgotten that American foreign policies over at least the past fifty years have not been wholly humanitarian and altruistic in nature. Some cited the hundreds of thousands of Iraqi children who died as a result of American bombing raids, as well as U.S.-backed economic sanctions. Others cited the United States' dual containment policies toward Iraq and Iran, which fueled the bloody eight-year-long Iran-Iraq War, in which the U.S. supported Saddam Hussein (by, among other things, approving and helping pay for Iraq's acquisition of biological and chemical weapons) and in which hundreds of thousands of Iraqis and Iranians were killed. Still others cited U.S. complicity with and tolerance of genocide in Rwanda and the former Yugoslavia, along with U.S. willingness to shed the blood of innocents abroad for the sake of attaining and retaining oil, weapons, sugar, and other material resources and commodities.

In short, the historical events I heard cited as evidence of the U.S. government's bad behavior abroad (some called it colonialism, others bad foreign policy, and still others terrorism) were varied and plenteous. By far the most commonly cited evidence, however, in some way referenced the billions of dollars that the U.S. government spends yearly in aid to the Israeli government and its racist policies. Israel is the top recipient of U.S. economic aid, receiving more than any other country in the world, despite its continued commitment to illegal occupation and its refusal to grant Palestinian refugees the right to return to their homelands.

As a Palestinian, Molham is no exception to this trend. When I ask him what he thinks of the outpouring of support for the Palestinian cause I had encountered among young Muslim Americans across cultures, races, and nationalities, he is indifferent at best.

"It's nice and all, but it isn't and shouldn't be a Muslim issue. It's a political issue that only gets worse when you bring religion into it. So many Palestinians are Christian anyway. Systems based on ethnicity and religion are inherently unfair. That's all there is to it. I find that American Jews who have never been to Israel are far more likely to support fanatical Zionist ideologies than Jews living in Israel. Many of the Israeli Jews I have met or known have in fact been vehemently against the occupation. They've seen it and lived it. It makes sense that they would be against it because they too have suffered its bloody consequences.

"We've got to stop letting the crazies on both sides do the negotiating. Just because they are yelling the loudest and doing the most outrageous things—like blowing up cafés or stealing someone else's house or bulldozing it while they are still in it—doesn't mean that anyone with half a brain who happens to also be Israeli or Palestinian actually thinks that stuff like that is OK. If we could just get some of the rational people from both sides together, I don't see how we couldn't work things out."

Molham is an almost annoyingly rational thinker. Each thought stems logically from the last—so much so that I don't doubt that I could map out his entire interview as a long line of successive syllogisms. We conducted our interview on a weeknight, in one of the many empty offices on the half floor that comprises the Atlanta office of Optimi, which Molham and a friend of his, also Palestinian, started up a couple of years ago. I still have no idea what all the numbers on the dry-erase boards in his offices mean, despite Molham's repeated attempts to explain them to me. I have gathered, however, that Optimi is a software company that writes programs for wireless operators. It has acquired three other companies since it started, and it made millions of dollars last year alone. Molham and his friend own 35 percent of the company, and the employees (130 people, half working here in the States and the other half in European offices) own the rest.

"I always said I would work until I was thirty-five and then retire, but I'm turning thirty-five in May. I'd love to maybe go back and finish my Ph.D. [in mathematics], but I definitely don't think I'm ready to retire. I guess some of it's my own personal greed, but mostly, I feel committed to the people I work with—to see things through to at least some reasonable conclusion. It would be wrong to stop now."

Molham is a complete workaholic. I met him through Salman (a family friend and the closest thing I've ever had to an older brother). Sal told me that he knew *of* Molham but that he had never met him personally. Apparently, Sal had crashed at his place when he was passing through Atlanta one night. Upon the insistence of a friend of a friend, he ended up staying in Molham's apartment while Molham was out of town on business. They still have never met, but as odd as it is, that was my initial connection. Were Molham not the kind of guy who would let a stranger crash at his place on a friend's recommendation, I would have never run into him. Lucky for me, Molham is loyal and trusting, and lucky for Molham, Sal is gracious, neat, and considerate. Through Molham, I began to realize just how simultaneously extended and familiar my friend-of-a-friend-of-a-friend selection process had become.

The last time Sal came to town, Matthew and I joined him and a bunch of his friends for dinner at some painfully trendy new restaurant. A friend of one of these friends was Molham's ex-girlfriend, and though she was sitting at the opposite end of the table from me, when I found out who she was, I indiscreetly made my way down to the other end of the table and sat beside her. Pretty and well dressed, she looked and acted like a lot of other women I have met since moving to Georgia, though I'm not sure whether she grew up here or not. Regardless, she had this air of Southern aristocracy about her that somewhat turned me off. Maybe she was wearing pearls? I don't remember.

At any rate, I sat down next to her, staring at her pale face with curiosity and purpose as I shook her hand and introduced myself. I think I startled her a little, but I didn't care. I was on a mission. I was still in the process of writing Molham's chapter, and I interpreted our meeting as fate. I immediately spilled the beans, telling her that I was interviewing Molham for a book and that I would be interested in getting her perspective on him.

I knew that whatever she said would have to be taken with a grain of salt, given that she was his *ex*-girlfriend, but ultimately, to my great surprise, there was no salt needed. All she had to say about Molham was that he was a sweet, kind, and fascinating man—but just too much of a workaholic for her. Big help you are, I thought to myself; I knew all of that within five minutes of meeting him. Still, she was somewhat helpful in that she confirmed my suspicion that Molham's charm and charisma were useful not only in picking up bright and attractive women but also in assuring the absence of any hard feelings once a relationship had run its course.

The ex was dead-on in her assessment of Molham as a workaholic. He has a strong sense of ambition and a serious work ethic, and I don't think that any woman without her own set of high personal ambitions could fully understand or tolerate him. Molham is uncompromisingly living out his version of the American dream, and if you can't respect that, it's likely you won't get along with him, as his enthusiasm and ambition might easily be mistaken for arrogance by those unwilling or unable to take a slightly closer look.

Molham laughs when I ask him how it feels to be living out the American dream, but soon he becomes serious: "This country really provides a lot of opportunities to make something out of nothing, to change things. I have this theory that the ideas that are better win—eventually at least, and this country is all about encouraging the best ideas. Beyond that, I honestly think the American system is in some ways the most evolved in terms of separating church and state and respecting individual freedoms to express different ideas. Sure, it's not perfect, but time and demographics are on my side here. The world is getting browner and browner, and America is on the forefront of that phenomenon. It's getting harder and harder to define ourselves by our differences."

✦✦✦ ✦✦✦

Molham is unimpressed by religion on its surface, as he has personally experienced its disastrous effects throughout his lifetime. More than anything, Molham's religion appears to be science and mathematics. Having always been daunted by numbers and formulas, and much more drawn to words and language, I am perpetually in awe of people like him. I have always felt that everyone has a unique lens through which she or he can best see God. My rationale lies in the firm belief that God couldn't be small enough to fit into one religion, field, or experience, that God's got to be bigger than that. Molham's lens is large parts calculus, physics, chemistry, and logic. Islam is definitely part of that lens, but considered in isolation, it appears to comprise a smaller part than science. But Molham does not consider Islam in isolation—it overlaps significantly with science and mathematics for him.

"The part of Islam that I relate to most is the part responsible for seven hundred years of scientific history that contributed so much to math, chemistry, physics, astronomy. It's frustrating that these contributions don't seem to make their way into most American classrooms. When Islam began it was about enlightenment. It empowered so many people who were oppressed at the time. I mean, it was essentially solely responsible for ending the regular practice of infanticide of female children throughout the Arab world. That was huge.

"My point is that when it began, Islam drew its strength, beauty, and appeal from progressive ideas. The best ideas won. We lost the entire plot when it [Islam] started to be less open to new ideas. My interpretation of Islam is more open and fair than what I see passing as Islam these days. I drink. I don't pray. I don't do a lot of stuff, but I believe in the story of Islam and its acknowledgment of the fact that God gave you a brain and you should use it. At the core, if I had to take the label off of my religion it just boils down to the golden rule for me, really. That and using your brain to advance humanity. I think that a lot of people use faith the wrong way—they use it as an excuse to be stupid or lazy instead of using it to incite education and self-improvement."

More than anyone or anything else, Molham credits his parents for any success he has achieved in his short life. Specifically, he credits the fact that they relentlessly encouraged and inspired him through their words and their actions to advance and develop his ideas in all of his studies and endeavors. "They always challenged me to do better, and as a result, I have a thing for going after hard problems and trying to solve them, and sometimes I actually do." As I write this, Molham is spending the week somewhere in France on business, attempting to do exactly that. I'd like to believe him that the best ideas always win out in the end, and if he's right (and believe me, he's the kind of guy who wants to be right), it looks like early retirement isn't in the cards for him. There are just way too many tough problems out there that no one has managed to solve yet, and I have no doubt that they weigh on him, that they keep him up some nights, challenging him to do better.

NINE

Willow

But those who believe
And work in righteousness—
No burden do We place
On any soul, but that
Which it can bear—
They will be the Companions
Of the Garden, therein
To dwell (forever).

And We shall remove
From their hearts any
Lurking sense of injury—
Beneath them will be
Rivers flowing—and they
Shall say: "Praise be to God,
Who hath guided us
To this (felicity): never
Could we have found
Guidance, had it not been
For the guidance of God:
Indeed it was the truth
That the Messengers of our Lord
Brought unto us." And they
Shall hear the cry:
"Behold the Garden before you!
Ye have been made
Its inheritors, for your
Deeds (of righteousness)."

—QUR'AN, AL A'RAF (THE ELEVATED PLACES,
OR THE HEIGHTS), 7:42–43

Well I left my happy home to see what I could find out
I left my folk and friends with the aim to clear my mind out
Well I hit the rowdy road and many kinds I met there
Many stories told me of the way to get there.

—YUSUF ISLAM (FORMERLY CAT STEVENS),
"ON THE ROAD TO FIND OUT"

In that brief moment between dialing the last digit and hearing the first ring, I began to sweat. That moment is always just a little bit longer on international calls, and on this particular call it seemed interminable. There was really no good reason for me to be so nervous, but I was. Perhaps it was the fact that Willow was the first person whom I wouldn't be interviewing face-to-face, or that she was a convert, or that she lived in Cairo, or that she wore *hijab*. Whatever the reason, I had managed to conjure a formidable sweatstache by the time her husband picked up the phone. I was glad he picked up because when I asked for her, my voice cracked. What was I, twelve? I imagined that this was what online dating was like and immediately thanked God that I got married before that whole phenomenon got so big. I wiped my sweatstache off with my sleeve and tried to chill out.

I had heard about Willow through a friend at *Parabola*, a sort of artsy quarterly religion journal devoted to "the search for meaning." An editor there had decided to publish an excerpt from this book for the magazine's Winter 2006 edition, and since then, he and I had become friends. So when I was looking for more "subjects," I immediately thought of him. When I asked if he knew anyone who might be appropriate, he at once recommended Willow. He sent me her e-mail address and wrote this above it: "You should contact G. Willow Wilson. She is an uber-cool young woman (28?) from Boulder, CO (whitey convert) who is now a journalist living in Cairo. Her graphic novel called 'Cairo' is coming out on Vertigo/DC comics next year and has the artist who inks 'Sandman' comics [M. K. Perker], therefore she is and will soon become very cool. Oh she's a hijabi [wears *hijab*]. She had an article in the latest PARABOLA [Fall 2006]. Tre good."

Tre good indeed. Maybe that's why I was sweating. I had read her article in *Parabola*, along with a piece she had published not too long before in the *Atlantic Monthly* and several other pieces she had linked to on her Web site. After googling her and reading absolutely everything she had written that I could get my hands on, I had come to the conclusion that she must be some sort of high-brow academic, sitting in some Egyptian ivory tower with an office full of Ph.D.'s hanging on the walls. She just sounded so damn *smart* in all of her writings. Not in an inaccessible, pretentious way, but in a way that made you think that this was somebody who lived in the realm of ideas and was consumed by meaningful thought. And who pays for that these days besides academia? This was the misguided logic I used in presuming her professorship. I really should have known better, though, having come across so many ignorant academics and brilliant "civilians" in the course of obtaining my higher education. Whatever the case, it was clear that, at the very least, this woman had her wits about her.

She sounded just as smart over the phone as she did in her writing, and I finally had to mute my stereo to give her my total undivided attention. She isn't the kind of person you can multitask with—you have to listen to everything, because if you don't, you'll be sure to miss something. You can ask your friends to repeat themselves, but you can't keep doing that when you're interviewing a stranger. It looks unprofessional. So I had to hit mute.

By the time I cut off Morrissey in the middle of *Satan Rejected My Soul*, I was still collecting basic stats: She was born on August 31, 1982, in New Jersey. She is roughly four years younger than my friend at *Parabola* had guessed. Her full name is Gwendolyn Willow Wilson, but she publishes under G. Willow Wilson and goes by the name Willow. She describes herself as quintessentially American: a mix of German, French, Scotch-Irish, English, and Italian heritage. Her parents are still together, and they both have liberal inclinations. As for religion, Willow notes, "My parents are an atheist and an agnostic with Protestant backgrounds, so I really don't in any way follow the religion of my parents, but I do follow their philosophy: Be nice at all costs. It's the best way to go through life."

She mentions spending a few years, when she was "super young," living with her parents on an organic farm, which apparently turned out to be far too much work, so that her mom and dad ultimately moved to Boulder and got "real" nine-to-five jobs in finance and telecommunications, respectively. "They wised up and joined the corporate armada," she declares with a hint of sarcasm. Still, Willow's hippie roots aren't at all a surprise, and not just because of her name. There's something very warm and ethereal about her voice, and her writing is bursting with progressive, revisionist, and ultimately restorative undertones, if not overtones. Being a convert of any variety tends to require that one be at once dangerously curious and a free thinker. Willow is undeniably both of these things, and I don't doubt that being raised by reformed hippies has something to do with this.

⁄⁄⁄ ⟩⟩⟩

Willow converted to Islam when she was twenty years old—in her last year of college at Boston University. She was studying Arabic and Middle Eastern studies, and in the course of her studies, she found herself reading the Qur'an.

In her words, "It was like getting hit in the head. . . . By the time I converted, I knew that I was going to convert for about a year beforehand. . . . Literally, the first time that I read the 'The Elevated Places, Surah Al A'raf' [the seventh *surah*, sometimes translated as 'The Heights'], I knew. I mean, I just read it, and I was like, I *have* to join this religion. And even though I sort of sat on that and let it develop for about a year, I knew almost immediately when I read the Qur'an that I would convert someday."

Willow couldn't have timed her conversion much more inauspiciously. She was living in Boston, not quite two years after 9–11, when this bombshell of a revelation "hit her in the head." Thus, her conversion was very private: "I didn't want to deal with all the fear and the questions, so I just didn't tell anybody. . . . I'd been trying to find ways around it [converting] because it was just such an inconvenient thing to do, but I couldn't."

Such "inconvenience" certainly characterizes any American's conversion to Islam, especially after 9–11. Nevertheless, practical "inconvenience" is a truth that spans the entirety of the Muslim American experience. Then again, isn't inconvenience a hallmark of all minority experiences? Certainly, it's harder, less "convenient," to be an African American, a Native American, or a Jew in the United States than it is to be part of the white Christian majority. There's no denying that some sense of human hardship unites all minority experiences, and these hardships can lead to very different results for different minority groups and individuals.

While some minorities embrace their unique race, religion, or nationality as a source of pride, others try desperately to hide it or "pass." Examples of the latter attempt to bury one's true identity are painfully prevalent in the U.S. They include Jews and other minorities changing any recognizably identifiable surnames, or immigrant parents choosing more "American"-sounding first names for their children, or the deep-seated preference for lighter skin lurking within many African American communities (a preference, incidentally, that is far from exclusive to African Americans, that is in fact rampant both in the U.S. and throughout the world among many communities of color). While many members of minority groups might find the idea of trying to pass, often by emulating one's oppressor or colonizer, revolting, others just see it as a way of simplifying their lives, their reasoning being, the less differently I look or behave, the less differently I will be treated. Generally this isn't so, but that doesn't mean people aren't still trying. There's a huge discount on cowardice and indolence for minorities in the United States, and unfortunately, all too frequently the allure of the bargain overrides that of honesty and integrity. I imagine that's why so many people still try to pass—for the simple fact that they can get away with it and that it just seems easier than the alternative.

Then there are people like Willow—doing the exact opposite. Those rare adventurous souls who follow their hearts wherever they may lead, to hell with the rest of the world. Refusing to deny the truth and comfort that she found in Islam some twenty years into her life, Willow willingly and intentionally dove headfirst into the multifaceted mess that is today's Muslim American experience. Any sort of active conversion requires a degree of courage and faith that I don't think most people have. This is what I find so fascinating about Willow and others like her. Willow happened to stumble upon the most persecuted religion in her homeland, and upon learning the truth about it, she not only tolerated but respected it. Then, she took this one step further when she realized that this faith happened to speak to her on a personal level. She converted.

Again, several factors unite minority experiences within the U.S., particularly the reality of hardship, but each minority experience also has something unique about it that distinguishes it from the others. For Muslim Americans, such distinguishing factors have grown exponentially since September 11, 2001 —not because the reality of their faith or beliefs has changed but because the Western perception of Islam has been so extremely influenced by radicalism, fundamentalism, the so-called War on Terror, and the disastrous American and British occupation of Iraq. It is impossible to talk about Willow's conversion without understanding the kind of world in which that conversion took place—perhaps unfortunate, but definitely true. In a time and place that could at best be described as overtly hostile to Islam, Willow did her own research and accepted Islam as her personal spiritual path.

While she describes her actual conversion as a very organic and natural progression, Willow does clearly remember the moment when she formally converted—that is, the moment when she took the *shahada*. The *shahada* is one's declaration of faith in Islam: a declaration made by all converts and repeated innumerable times in prayers, contemplations, and even everyday speech by all kinds of Muslims. Specifically, the *shahada* consists of saying, and truly believing, the following words:"La ilaha il Allah, Muhammad-ur-Rasool-Allah." There is only one God, and that is Allah [the God of the Abrahamic tradition], and Muhammad was his messenger. Many converts take the *shahada* for the first time inside of a mosque, wherein a celebration generally ensues. This was not the case with Willow. Her conversion was a very quiet and private one, and thus, her celebration occurred where all the best celebrations do: within her heart.

"I guess for a couple of days before [taking the *shahada*] I was sort of thinking about my future and what I wanted to do and where I wanted to go, and it was terrifying to me to think of, you know, adult life sort of opening up in front of me . . . like a chasm: nothing is set for you anymore. . . . It was scary, but at the same time it was sort of exhilarating, and I was like, 'OK, I want to be on my path now.' You know, I'm ready. *Now* I'm ready to take the *shahada*. So I did say the *shahada*, and I remember saying it. And so the next week after that, I was thinking in the back of my mind, 'God, I'm a Muslim. Geez, I'm a Muslim.' It was really weird."

Initially, Willow didn't tell anybody about her conversion, but she soon realized that it wasn't something she could keep to herself. Her motivation behind trying to keep it to herself, moreover, had less to do with others' potential shock and disapproval than with her experience of Islam as a deeply private and intimate affair. Thus, fittingly, her impetus to "come out" as a Muslim lay in another deeply private and intimate affair: her marriage. Conversions, baptisms, deaths, and marriages are some of our most intimate human experiences, and yet humans always seem to be trying to make big public spectacles out of them. Willow, however, is not one for such spectacles, and she lives her life accordingly. After graduating from BU, she moved to Cairo to experience her new faith more fully by living in a majority Muslim country. Almost a year after her conversion, while in Cairo, she met her husband, Omar.

"When I met Omar . . . I knew that when we decided to get married . . . that I would have to tell people [that I had become Muslim]. Otherwise, it would come out in a situation over which I had no control and people would assume that I had done it for him, and I didn't want that."

Willow met Omar at Misr Language School, a private English-language high school in Cairo, where they both taught. She is now freelancing as a writer, and he is freelancing as a translator. While "freelancing" can mean a lot of things to a lot of different people, Willow takes it very seriously. Since she can remember, she has always wanted to write. She writes at least a thousand words every day, and she's damn good at it. At the age of twenty-two, Willow wrote a revealing piece about the Grand Mufti of Egypt, Ali Gomaa, called "The Show-Me Sheikh," and published it in the *Atlantic Monthly*.[1] Publishing in the *Atlantic Monthly* or *Harper's* is a fairly common dream for just about every struggling American writer. And for someone to do it at twenty-two, without a stack of Ph.D.'s or a gazillion prestigious prior publications, is not just incredible—it's downright annoying.

On top of that, there's that part about her being the first Muslim woman to write for a mainstream American comics publisher, namely Vertigo, an imprint of DC Comics (renowned for its Superman and Batman comics). The graphic novel *Cairo*, which she wrote and M. K. Perker illustrated, is due out in September 2007. While she engages in many different kinds of writing, Willow insists that comics are her favorite. She has a knack for satire, and I don't doubt that this is part of what drew her to comics in the first place. From what I've heard from those in the know (excluding Willow, who seems to only talk about it, or any of her other accomplishments, for that matter, under extreme duress), *Cairo* promises to be a hit.

Being in the same perpetually mortifying line of work, Willow and I share a similar sense of skepticism that some might view as cynicism. Still, she manages to be a good deal less jaded than I as far as I can discern, and perhaps that is what I most envy about her. It's not her collection of publications as much as her determined equipoise and determination when it comes to the craft of writing. For me, writing is often considerably agonizing, but I can't seem to stop doing it, partly because I don't see certain important things being said and I know of no other way to say them, and partly because there are things about the process that I do enjoy—but again, the great majority of it is still incredibly excruciating for me, and this translates into ever-increasing and more elaborate modes of procrastination.

Willow somehow manages to devote herself to writing as she would any other more conventional profession. This consistency and dedication seriously intrigue me, as I have never had, nor do I anticipate ever having, that kind of self-discipline. Willow doesn't seem like the kind of person who would set out to write and then end up buying a pair of completely impractical Versace stilettos online instead. I, on the other hand, *am* that person and hence perpetually in awe of the consistent and focused Willows of the world, with their unwavering work ethic and their sensible shoes. For me at least, when confronted with writers who fall into this annoyingly conscientious category, I have to settle for admiration or resentment, and I generally veer toward the latter, often peppering it with flawed and grandiose rationalizations about writing being an *art* and therefore somehow above the rigors of order and discipline. Willow, however, makes resentment pretty impossible, given her friendliness, her self-deprecation, her gregariousness, and her rare and surprisingly sincere eagerness to help a sister out.

Upon recognizing my apparent awe, Willow immediately offered to help me in any way she could, writer to writer. How *could* I hate her? She was like one of those adorable little six-year-old virtuosos rocking Tchaikovsky on the violin, as if it were as easy as peeling a banana, on NPR's *From the Top*. I tend to have a similar reaction when confronted with such people—half of me wants to wring their necks, and the other half wants to sit and watch them for days to see if it's all for real. To make sure that they're not all robots, like the girl in that stupid 1980s sitcom *Small Wonder*, who had to recharge in some sort of upright coffin-looking thing every so often. Seeing as how I'm not headed to Cairo any time soon, it'll be a while before I can fully substantiate that Willow is indeed not a robot, but all the evidence I have thus far gathered seems to point toward her being 100 percent human. Still, not being able to fully confirm or deny this, I have chosen to accept the high improbability of her being a robot. As a result, I have settled for respect and admiration. Like I said, she's just too downright kind and agreeable to hate.

While Willow has worked hard for her achievements, she also admits that she has led a pretty blessed life. She has made quite a success of herself, and she knows it. Side note: when I say "success" here and throughout, even "professional success," I am referring not to monetary wealth but to a realization of one's goals—basic self-satisfaction, following one's bliss, that sort of thing. Essentially, income factors very minimally into my definition of "success." I wouldn't want to give the false impression that writers actually make any money—because most of us, even some of the more recognizable ones, don't. Economically, as a profession, it's pretty much up there with painting and panhandling. Turning a profit writing is like getting a telemarketer to hang up on you. It rarely happens. That said, Willow attributes much of her success, both personally and professionally, to her upbringing, and particularly to being American.

"I don't think I knew what that [being American] meant until I left the States. You know, I didn't realize what it meant to be American until I wasn't surrounded by other Americans. I like being American. . . . I feel like growing up in the States has given me tremendous, tremendous opportunities to be— I don't know—to become a fully realized person really. The U.S. is so big; it's large; it's insulated, and you feel really sort of like you're in a womb—like you can develop and be safe, and that's something cool.

"It's got good points and bad points. You know, I feel like a lot of Americans, and certainly me before I came here, are very out of touch with the rest of the world, sort of on a human level, because we're such a big country, and we're very prosperous, and we're very isolated. You know, the idea that everybody must want x, y, and z, or everybody must want this and that, and it's really not true. But I wouldn't be anything else really. I've never wanted to run away."

Willow didn't go to Cairo to escape from the United States or the prevalent misconceptions about Islam that have been plaguing the country as of late. Those who mattered in her life were accepting, enlightened, understanding people. Her close friends weren't really surprised when she informed them about her conversion. One of them told her, "Anyone who didn't see this coming wasn't paying attention." As for her parents, she says, "If they freaked out about my conversion, they were very good about keeping it to themselves."

Thus, Willow didn't really have anything worth "running away" from in the U.S.—her friends and family were enormously supportive of her in all her endeavors. While she anticipated shock and disapproval from some of those outside of her inner circle, she knew that she wouldn't have to spend any time enlightening her friends and family. Rather, she knew that the most she would have to do was perhaps occasionally *remind* them of just how enlightened they already were. And as for the yet-to-be-enlightened rest of the country, she seems to have faith that they will come around eventually, and even if they don't, she isn't the kind of person who worries all that much about what strangers might think of her.

On being a Muslim and an American, Willow has this to say: "To me they're inseparable. They're both outgrowths of a more essential identity: of Willow. I am a Muslim and an American. Politically this is incredibly irritating, but it's not an identity crisis. Philosophically, emotionally, America and Islam are part of who I am. Within me they don't conflict. . . . I imagine a lot of my [current] daily routines and expectations as a Muslim [living in Egypt] will have to be reimagined to fit into mainstream America. It's my country, though, so I don't mind making compromises for it."

Willow has no plans to leave Cairo at the moment. She genuinely loves it there. Nevertheless, her family is still in Colorado, and she is highly and unabashedly American. Some ex-pats, particularly Americans, can be painfully obnoxious and self-righteous in their desire to adopt and adapt to new and "exotic" cultures and customs. Willow, however, is not one of these ex-pats—in fact, I have great doubts as to whether "ex-patriot" is even a proper designation for her. Willow is more of an American patriot than most Americans who happen to live inside U.S. borders. When she says she wouldn't want to be anything other than American, she means it. She has a very clear and strong connection to the United States, and while she appreciates Egyptian culture and traditions, she has no desire or intention to be Egyptian. Ultimately, Willow hopes that she and her husband will divvy their time somewhat evenly between the U.S. and Egypt.

"Culture," Willow notes, "goes bone-deep, but there is something deeper than bone. It's vital to remember this if you're going to hopscotch between civilizations. I've learned it mostly the hard way, but it's the most valuable lesson I've taken away from my experience as an American Muslim."

/// \\\

Willow went to Egypt because she's a naturally curious person—a sort of modern embodiment of rugged individualism, with a new, unique, noncolonial spiritual interpretation of Manifest Destiny. I'm certain that she would dispute this analogy. What she wouldn't dispute, however, is that she wanted to fully experience another culture and way of life by going to Egypt, particularly one in which Islam plays such a large part. There is a unique sort of curiosity that white American converts, at least the ones I have come across, appear to share. It's not the kind of greedy, manipulative curiosity that tends to characterize colonialists and foreign investors. It's a genuine, childlike curiosity: something I think has been beaten out of most of us by the time we reach adolescence. Willow has it; Matthew has it.

I don't see the same innocent curiosity in African American converts—in them I see something far more familiar in its place: a search for justice, acceptance, and a faith that not only encourages but commands its adherents to fight back in the face of oppression and injustice. What I find common among both black *and* white American converts, however, is a profound understanding of the power of education. Still, the white Americans tend to retain this peculiar and unique curiosity—some might call it naïveté—generally uninterrupted by broader social structures and realities.

I realize that this is a substantial generalization, for which I am unaware of any supporting statistical data, but it is true to my personal experience, and it makes me wonder. I'm completely clueless as to how so many white American converts manage to maintain such an unsuspecting and benign curiosity. They grew up in the same world as I did, but somehow they can parse out curiosity from disdain, something I can't really remember ever being able to do. Perhaps it's because I've always been suspicious of those who were curious about *me*. The most obvious distinctions between me and Willow or Matthew seem to be my closer association with a foreign land (namely, Iran) and my skin color. I figure that those in the racial and cultural majority have the benefit of learning without judgment a little longer than those of us who fall within the minority because of such distinctions. The most I've learned to expect from those in the majority is tolerance, and I've never been too overjoyed at the prospect of having to be merely *tolerated*.

Still, this is my base expectation, and hence, when an apparent member of the majority is interested in my "background," I am immediately suspicious. Until I reached Wesleyan (hands down the most liberal and accepting place I have ever resided), it baffled me that any white American (man or woman) could actually find me attractive. As a general rule, when I was growing up in Ohio, whenever I heard a white American tell me that I was pretty, the compliment always seemed to end with an implicit or sometimes even explicit qualifier: *for a dark girl*. So, my guess as to why white American converts tend to keep this genuinely sweet sense of curiosity: they haven't been victims of the more insidious kind of curiosity that plagues the adult world. I could be way off, but that's my guess. Whatever the reason, though, Willow and Matthew definitely still have this delicious curiosity, and I definitely don't.

What's cool about Willow, though, is that she gets this distinction. Even from the outside, she can recognize it, and that has everything to do with her living in exile. She notes that when she first moved to Egypt, she "stuck out like crazy," such that everyone knew she wasn't Egyptian. As her Arabic has improved, however, she has found that she doesn't stick out quite as much, but she still doesn't quite fit in either.

"I'm like tragically white, you know, blue-eyed and the whole thing. At the beginning I would get stares everywhere I went. You know, constant, constant staring. I remember the first time I came here—I visited during my spring break of senior year in college—I broke out in hives in the middle of this crowded market in Luxor from the stress of all the negative attention. I don't stick out as much as I used to . . . but it's humbling. I think that everybody, every person who has the privilege of being in the majority of whatever country they live in, needs to get out and be in the minority for a while because it's just so incredibly eye-opening."

Willow, then, has an extremely rare combination of unfettered childlike curiosity and intense personal understanding of what it's like to be in the minority. "And yet," Willow adds, "I recognize that even when I am in a minority, I am in a privileged minority. White privilege definitely travels. All the white people who read this are going to roll their eyes, but I don't care; it's a reality, and you don't realize it until it follows you across the world. I get stared at and jeered at and insulted (people tell me this is a new phenomenon; Egypt used to be a more tolerant country, but oppression, poverty, and fundamentalism have done their work), but not openly discriminated against. In fact, I am often given more rights than the average Egyptian—certainly more room to break the rules—simply because of the color of my skin. It is a bizarre, bizarre paradox. I have to remind myself that while I am in Egypt I don't deserve anything an Egyptian does not have, and in this way give some of that privilege up. It's harder than it sounds; it means doing a lot of manual labor and standing in a lot of lines! But it's worth it for a clear conscience."

It's not often you meet someone who admits that she has an inherent unfair advantage, and it's even rarer to meet someone who is trying her best to shed that advantage in order to gain a new perspective on the world. Of course, you can't exactly just shed your whiteness, any more than you can shed your tallness. But Willow recognizes this, and she is doing her best to learn as much as she can from her current circumstances. This odd mix of recognition and eagerness to learn, which supersedes any desire to maintain preferential treatment, is certainly an incredibly rare blend, and this is part of what I find most endearing about Willow.

She also recognizes that she has had the added advantage of initially learning about Islam through its texts, of her own volition, at a time when she was old enough to understand them. This advantage escapes so many of those born into Muslim families, a reality that has led to some *huge* misunderstandings within Muslim communities—simply because people are too lazy to check things out for themselves. Instead, many of those born into the faith often just accept whatever they're told as if it were irrefutable fact. Hence, the seemingly endless passage of fictions from one generation to the next. As a result, those who have grown up in the faith often mistake cultural realities for religious ones.

Willow didn't absorb any of these false notions growing up, and because of that I feel like she really gets it. "The reality of God," she states, "is so massive that we cannot possibly begin to comprehend. All we have is the meager approximations of language. That's the thing for me that I find most frustrating with a lot of other religious people . . . they keep trying to shrink God." Willow isn't part of this seemingly ever-expanding God-shrinking posse, so often responsible for a disgusting manipulation of faith and so-called fundamentalism, which not so incidentally seems to be occurring across the board and not just in the allegedly "Islamic" world. Willow has also had the distinct advantage or disadvantage (depending on your perspective) of starting off with mature reason and a relatively clean slate. I can't help but see this as a huge advantage, but then again, the grass does tend to be at least a little bit greener on the other side.

✦✦✦

Once Willow actively chose Islam as her spiritual path, she dove right in. She is fully observant, to the extent that I imagine any human being can be fully observant. Like Ameer, she does things by the book: she prays five times a day, fasts, gives alms, plans on taking her pilgrimage, and most importantly believes. In addition, she chooses to wear *hijab* as an expression of her modesty. She's pretty distinctive about this, though, as she is about most things, and she doesn't consider it a requirement of the faith but rather her chosen personal articulation of it.

Willow began the piece she published in *Parabola* ("Arguing in Mecca") with a largely private debate over how to wear the *hijab* on one particularly hot morning. Her husband, whom she described to me as "a wonderful Egyptian man . . . intelligent, passionate, kind, and responsible," was a mere bystander in this debate. And it is a tribute to his intelligence that he got involved only minimally and then just to reassure her, as telling a woman how to wear her *hijab* or that she is wearing it "incorrectly" is in many ways the Islamic equivalent of telling an American woman that she looks fat in those jeans. Best to stay out of it.

"Nowhere in the *Qur'an*," she wrote, citing herself, "are pins [apparently customary to the Egyptian interpretation of *hijab*] mentioned. Nowhere in the *Hadith* are pins mentioned. I'm sick of pins. . . . It's my head. . . . Pins serve no religious purpose whatsoever. It's too hot to wear anything that tight. I'm not going to pin my scarf. I'm just going to drape it. Like Benazir [Bhutto]."

It is in these small rebellions against inconsequential customs, falsely assigned religiosity, that the magnificent universality of Islam emerges, and yet, it is also in these seemingly inconsequential customs that much of the beautiful diversity within Islam surfaces. A bit of a catch-22, but what isn't with Islam today? We're accused of being violent, for example, and then provoked with everything from cartoons to occupation. Then, a few of us give in and fulfill the terms of the accusation out of natural human desperation. And then the rest of us—the great majority of us, for whom violence is not a viable option or solution—get pinned with the rep. And we all know that a man's reputation precedes him; it's all he's got, right? So where does that leave us?

As Willow notes in the same piece, "It was barely nine o'clock in the morning, and it had taken an act of religious dissent and an invocation [her husband telling her 'Allahu ma'ik,' or 'God is with you'] just to get me out the door."

Willow is certainly not the only one arguing with herself, and pins are just the tip of the iceberg.

TEN

Hafeeza

And those to whom
Knowledge has come see
That the (Revelation) sent down
To thee from thy Lord—
That is the Truth
And that it guides
To the Path of the Exalted
(In Might), Worthy
Of all praise.

—QUR'AN, SABA (SHEBA), 34:6

I have never let my schooling interfere with my education.

—MARK TWAIN

Trying to get a straight, earnest answer out of Hafeeza is like trying to get a cat to bark. It just isn't happening. Even today, after knowing her for over a year in what most would call a friendly capacity, I still couldn't say for sure, for example, whether she adores or detests me, and neither would surprise me much. The girl is about as easy to read as a politician but lacks any of the caution, pretense, or diplomacy.

In the middle of our interview, she gets a text message—Hafeeza is obsessed with text messages. Her voicemail message announces, "You've reached Hafeeza. Please text-message me. If not, feel free to leave a message." Every time I leave a message, I feel guilty for forcing her to hear a human voice when writing is preferred, and I am pretty sure that this is her intent. This message is from Daran, whom she describes as "a magazine at the bus stop. It keeps you entertained for the time being, while you're waiting for another bus." As usual, I can't quite tell whether she's kidding or serious and eventually conclude, as usual, that she's just a little bit of both. I can't imagine that being so consistently ambivalent would be anything short of exhausting, but for Hafeeza it seems easy, natural, and even vitalizing.

Hafeeza grew up in Woodinville, Washington, a small, predominantly white upper-middle-class suburb about thirty miles outside of Seattle. Her family moved there from New Haven, where she was born, when Hafeeza was seven years old. While she speaks fondly of her family, she is less than enthusiastic about her classmates.

"Kids got drunk on the weekdays, smoked weed and snorted cocaine on the weekends, then returned to school to achieve the requisite A and do it all over again. Although I did not partake in the drugs or the alcohol—out of a direct, unacknowledged result of being raised Muslim—I loved being around the 'cool' kids, watching the partiers from the wall, even if I wasn't really one of them. And I wasn't. I had nappy hair that I stupidly tried to straighten with a relaxer. Inevitably, my hair looked ever crazier in a highly successful attempt to rebel. I have dark, deep brown skin; I am tall [five-foot-nine] and was very athletic—so what I'm trying to say is that I was a tall lanky black girl with crazy hair; the antithesis of all desirable features in a WASP high school such as mine.

"It didn't help that I was raised Muslim, which provided me with this seemingly unpronounceable name Hafeeza. It's phonetic. That's it. Yet everybody wants to say Afeesa or Aveeza or—what my neighbor called me for eight years—Hafreesia. Her name was Mrs. Katurnuik (pronounced Kat-er-nik), and she thought my name was difficult to say. Whatever. Where was I? Yes, there was me: an insult to the white Western standards of beauty. And of course my brothers—I have two older brothers—were the forbidden dream-come-true of every white girl, and either the envy or scorn of every white boy. So where does a black Black girl fit in? Yes, just as I said in the beginning . . . on the wall of the party watching the partiers drink, smoke, snort up, and rejuvenate. Ahh, high school. I was so happy to leave."

///   \\\

When I first met Hafeeza, she had just graduated from Spelman with a major in political science and was training to teach in the fall as part of the Americorps Teach for America program, which places top college graduates in underserved public school districts in desperate need of teachers. Matthew, being in the same program, insisted that I meet her and that we would get along great. His main initial selling points were the following: (1) she's funny, (2) she's beautiful, and (3) she's smart—in that order. So we met, and he was right. Still, we have not since become the close friends my husband was so sure we would, likely due in equal parts to our mutual laziness and to her genuine sense of contentment. Hafeeza appears to be content with the friends she already has, the person she already is, and the life she already lives. Despite appearances, however, she does acknowledge room for improvement. Like most everyone, Hafeeza would like to change more than a few things in her life that she has not quite yet gotten around to. Top on that list, moreover, sits Islam.

Hafeeza's Islamic heritage is newer than many others'. Her parents, who have been married for over thirty years, met when they were both students at Stanford. Her father, Haazim, had initial ambitions of becoming a Baptist minister. His father, with only a third-grade education, and his mother, with only an eighth-grade education, both strongly stressed the value of education to their three sons, including Haazim. Their wish was to make a doctor, a lawyer, and a minister out of their sons, and Haazim was poised to become the minister. Haazim, however, as Hafeeza puts it, "was put off by racism within the church, and he didn't very much jive with the images of this white Jesus." Thus, her father eventually converted to the Nation of Islam while at Stanford, and her mother followed suit soon after.

Hafeeza explains, "It was a time of a burgeoning black consciousness and pride in the black man and woman and the black community, and I think that was just attractive to them." Not long after joining the Nation of Islam, however, Hafeeza's parents opted to begin following traditional Islam instead. In doing so, they were in esteemed company. While Malcolm X began his path toward Islam under much less favorable conditions than the Rasheds—during six and a half years spent as an inmate in Massachusetts's Charlestown State Prison—he took a similar trajectory, first converting to the Nation and then later choosing the path of traditional Islam.

There is a widespread perception among many Americans, including many Muslim Americans, that the Nation of Islam is a racist and fanatical kind of cult, given its roots in radical, reactionary black separatism. While this explanation may be a simple one, as with most simple explanations, it is simply wrong. The Nation of Islam (NOI) was founded in 1930 by Wallace Fard Muhammad (who appointed Elijah Muhammad as his divine representative), and the sect was initially based on notions of black power and black separatism, but since then, the Nation of Islam has moved ideologically closer to more traditional Sunni Islam.

Still, many Muslims shun NOI as a purely political and social movement that uses Islam only when it is convenient to do so and ignores some of its basic tenets, especially concerning racial equality. Such determinations are highly un-Islamic, however, as Islam teaches that only God is the suitable judge of His followers and that Muslims must greet and accept other self-proclaimed Muslim brothers and sisters as such (4:94). Both Islam and NOI (as well as many other religions, for that matter) have been used to achieve political ends, and both with limited success; both evolved in opposition to oppression, and both have roots in slavery. While the differences are many and should not be ignored, they should neither be exaggerated.[1]

Having been born into a Muslim family, Hafeeza explains, "I haven't really considered another religion. I have been exposed a great deal to many religions, but none ever called to me like Islam. I like that Islam is rather rigid in its applications. You either are a Muslim or you're not. To be a Muslim, you follow five seemingly simple rules: (1) declare faith, (2) pray five times a day, (3) pay *zakat*, (4) fast during the month of Ramadan, and (5) go to Mecca if you can afford to at least once in your lifetime. If you don't fulfill one of these, then you're basically out of the club. Everything else comes after. Now those are some guidelines people can follow.

"I'm a second-grade teacher, and kids are only capable of following rules that are short and simple. I have a mind to think that Allah is a second-grade teacher to His children: there are just five rules, and no one has disputed them. Unlike with the *hijab*. Unlike with the alleged teachings of the Prophet, may peace and blessing be upon him [referring to the Sunnah, which constitute the collected sayings and actions of the Prophet Muhammad, many of which are highly disputed as to their legitimacy]. How simple, right?

"Now as far as the application goes, though, I resemble my second-grade students: I forget these rules, lash out, try to follow them, try to reinterpret them though I know the meaning, and basically do everything but follow them. Just like my students, sometimes I follow them to a T, but most of the time I slip. And Allah, just as every second-grade teacher across the country, has clear-cut consequences. But in the midst of the day, I take no heed and continue along as though the dismissal bell will never ring. But it always does. For every day."

Given her interpretation, it's understandable that Hafeeza refers to herself as a "Muslim wannabe," but I'm afraid that if Hafeeza's definition of what it is to be a Muslim is in fact correct, then it may very well be the case that only the Prophet Muhammad himself would qualify. Still, I understand her rationale. Adhering to the pillars of Islam is mandatory for those who call themselves Muslims, but perhaps these are not so much "rules" as they are indispensable building blocks for the making of a good Muslim. Moreover, it seems beneath God to line us all up at the gates of heaven with a checklist. The anthropomorphization of God leads to some rather ridiculous images and conclusions, but despite the fact that most people who believe in some form of Greater Being or Force would deny that It is anything close to human, most people still envision God as such. Perhaps there is no way to fully escape this tendency, but I am convinced that it is this human penchant for knowing and understanding through relation, not only to human nature, but even more specifically to oneself, is responsible for this trap. I bring up this trap only because I am about to fall headfirst into it and wish to apologize in advance.

Hafeeza's depiction of Islam paints God as an omniscient and omnipresent Referee, calculating our grades based on effort, behavior, and achieved results, much as Hafeeza grades her pupils. A more apt depiction, however, might be that of an almighty Coach in a game where no one ever wins but where the level of the game is the only concern. In many ways, a coach isn't focusing solely on the score—rather, he is looking at how his players are approaching the game and how they might alter their strategy to improve that game. While Hafeeza may envision a God that more resembles a referee than a coach, her experiences indicate that God's role in her life has been that of a guide and supporter, rather than that of a scowling disciplinarian.

Hafeeza knows that she isn't a perfect Muslim, but unlike most of us—

who are equally aware of our imperfections and still freely identify ourselves as such through our words, actions, dress, and/or beliefs—Hafeeza has too much respect for the faith and for those who are more observant than she to allow herself to freely and unqualifiedly identify herself as Muslim. While if asked, she is always quick to say that she is Muslim and takes pride in the tenets of her faith, I have never heard Hafeeza discuss her connection to Islam without some form of qualification. In effect, she tends to say things like, "Yes, I am a Muslim, but I am not yet a *real* Muslim." I would argue that she, like so many of all faiths, is simply not yet as close to God as she can be or wants to be. The fact that she can't comfortably and unqualifiedly refer to herself as a Muslim points as much to her humility, her faith, and her belief in the human capacity to realize ideals as it does to her present lapses in practice.

Any apparent unease or hesitancy associated with discussing her personal relationship with God, however, vanishes when the topic turns to American interpretations of Islam, and Hafeeza's standard sarcastic tone returns immediately. "Americans' views of Islam? What, that Islam was created to birth, preen, and mold terrorists? That thinking is preposterous and frankly ridiculous. It really shows how little America discusses colonialism and imperialism and basically world history. Or even the world. Because the so-called terrorists, wherever they exist, are fighting for Islam the same way the British were fighting for Christianity. And we all know how that turned out. It was bogus. A thin hijab to disguise the real pursuit of power. A justification for violent and questionable means. But America only really discovered Muslims in 2001. Even though Islam has been around for over a millennium, Americans were hearing strange words like 'Qur'an,' 'Allah,' and 'Muhammad' for the first time. I just have to shake my head. . . . And what do I take comfort in as an American Muslim? That I'm black. And unfortunately, black people have always been invisible, always seemed to have 'weird' names, so no one ever makes the association between Hafeeza Rashed and terrorist. Simply because I am a black Black woman."

As a "black Black woman," Hafeeza may not be subject to the same stereotypes as Middle Easterners, Arabs, or Pakistanis, for example—most notably that of "terrorist"—but she has, however, been subject to the equally immediate and superficial stereotypes associated with being a particularly dark African American woman, or more specifically with being what she calls a "black Black woman." Hafeeza's most vivid memory of elementary school after moving to the Pacific Northwest is that of several children asking her, "Are you from Africa?" to which she proudly remembers consistently responding, "Are you from

Europe?" She was one of two black children in a school of six hundred, and that experience as a super-minority had more than a little to do with her choice to travel across the country for college.

At Spelman, Hafeeza was surprised to find that she apparently spoke English, her native tongue, with an "accent." This statement puzzles me, as she speaks no differently than I do, and no one has ever told me I have an accent. Then she begins to explain: "My parents are Stanford and Yale graduates. My mother is the child of two physicians, and she grew up in California. My father may have been born in Tennessee, but he lived in upstate New York and Germany. On top of that, I was raised in Washington State. As a result, I've been told that my diction is a bit crisp or, in layman's terms, 'white.'"

This begins to make sense, and I can understand what she's getting at. Given my dubious shade, I have on more than one occasion been mistaken for being African American—that is, when I'm not being mistaken for a Latina, Jew, Indian, or Italian, among other things. In my experiences being mistaken for an African American, however, I have periodically been chastised by near-total strangers within the African American community for acting or talking too white and, most commonly by African American men, for marrying, dating, or even just holding hands with a conspicuously white man. Generally, I correct the misconception and am left alone at once, but I have now and then assumed my mistaken identity, and I must admit that every experiment in doing so has led to unfavorable results, generally entailing extensive profanity and concluding with one of my customary and ever so grown-up final declarations in such circumstances: "Fuck you," "Screw you," or "Bite me." Hafeeza's preferred response to comments regarding her "whiteness," however, tends to take the more civil and innocuous form of laughter, followed by her signature sarcastically disapproving glare.

Hafeeza spent eight months in Africa when she was in college, dividing that time equally between Ghana and Botswana. Nowhere in Africa did anyone accuse her of "being white"—partly because different cultural hang-ups made race a nonissue, according to Hafeeza. With most Africans being black, there was little notion of "whiteness." Whatever impression of whiteness remained from colonialism was not nearly as overtly pejorative within the black African community as it apparently tends to be within the African American community. In Africa, Hafeeza was able to see how truly American she is—completely irrespective of the issue of race.

"I'm American," Hafeeza explains, "in the sense that I buy my food totally prepared instead of cooking. I talk to my dog like she is a human, and she lives indoors. I have my own car and drive it to the grocery store less than a mile away from my home. Occasionally I walk, but not often. I wear jeans even when it's too cold or too hot. I love, love, love 'me-time,' which is really anti-social time, which if you think about it is like antihuman because if everybody insisted on 'me-time' as much as American psychologists encourage us to, the fabric of society would just rip—not tear but literally rip—apart. Where was I? Oh, and I have way too many choices, which essentially causes me to refrain from doing anything. Because when you have too much choice—should I eat hamburgers, burritos, palak paneer, or falafels for dinner?—your brain just shuts down and you don't choose anything. That's why our government just doesn't do it for me. And that's why Americans like GW [George W. Bush]. We—well, privileged Americans like me—just have so many choices in our lives that Bush's 'do-it-my-way-or-die' attitude is like—refreshing." She ends this tirade laughing in disapproval, but there's more.

"Oh, and it also helps that every time I leave the country I can literally *feel* my Americanness seeping out of me. It has a pungent smell and causes foreigners to wrinkle their noses and scratch their heads when it is emitted, right about the same time that I am either doing or saying something horribly inappropriate. It's only when I step outside of American borders that I realize just how truly American I am."

At present, sitting in my living room after eating the dinner I cooked to lure her here, Hafeeza smells like *kalam polo*, an Iranian dish consisting of rice, meat, cabbage, and buckets of tarragon. After her amusing metaphor about the smell of her Americanness giving her away, I wonder if I should tell her that her sweat is likely to reek of tarragon for the next few days at least. Ultimately, I decide to keep quiet and preserve the mystery of this new culinary experience for her own firsthand personal discovery. In many ways, it is our own unique individual experiences living and growing in this country that help distinguish, define, and elevate the distinct, varied nature of any true American experience. I would never want to deny a fellow American the novelty, the privilege, or the surprise of a new, unique, individual experience unfettered by the warnings or preconceptions of others.

ELEVEN

Asra

Not equal are those
Believers who sit (at home)
And receive no hurt,
And those who strive
And fight in the cause
Of God with their goods
And their persons.
God hath granted
A grade higher to those
Who strive and fight
With their goods and persons
Than to those who sit (at home).
Unto all (in Faith)
Hath God promised good:
But those who strive and fight
Hath He distinguished
Above those who sit (at home)
By a special reward—

Ranks specially bestowed
By Him and Forgiveness
And Mercy, for God is
Oft-Forgiving, Most Merciful.

—Qur'an, Al Nisa (The Women), 4:95–96

I am glad to see that men are getting their rights,
But I want women to get theirs, and while the water is
stirring I will step into the pool.

—Sojourner Truth

I've never felt so concurrently welcome and unwelcome in a single moment as I did within a day of meeting Asra. Sitting on the floor of her hometown mosque in Morgantown, West Virginia, where her father had helped establish the town's first mosque, I could feel the hate and hostility in the air tightening around my heart like a steel clamp. Asra sat directly beside me in the middle of this vast carpeted space, with three evenly spaced chandeliers hanging from the ceiling and a hollering Egyptian cardiologist standing on a raised platform in the front of the room, preaching absurdity after absurdity. On that rainy day, we sat amid a sea of men, none of whom seemed to care for our company.

I wore the long chador I always keep in my car with my prayer rug on the off chance that I find the need or inspiration to pray while on the road. It has tons of tiny red flowers on it that are indiscernible from any reasonable distance, and when I wear it, only my face and my feet are visible. Asra wore jeans and a loose black windbreaker from her volleyball days that read "Six Pack" on the back, in white letters. On her head, she wore a gift I had given her the night before: a pink baseball cap with "Allah" embroidered in bright white Arabic letters on the front. She loved the hat and wore it proudly throughout my visit. It suits her perfectly, as she is in many ways a sort of cheerleader for the compatibility of Islam, women's rights, and American ideals. She loves her respective teams and doesn't mind being an underdog. In fact, she seems to thrive on it.

Her spirit and nerve are downright infectious—so much so that being around her for any significant period of time promises to make an activist out of even the most complacent soul. A woman like that is dangerous on so many levels to so many people, and that's why, I imagine, so many people have tried to shut her up. But she's not shutting up, and not only is she not shutting up; she's inspiring others to speak up through her example.

Looking back, I realize that it was largely Asra's contagious courage that drove me to accompany her on her weekly journey into the confines of what was for me the new and foreign land of the men's section of the mosque. Every American mosque I have ever visited has been segregated by sex. Women are either in the back, in a separate room, or on a balcony, while men generally reign over a sizable main hall. This type of segregation is conspicuously absent in Mecca, the holiest city of Islam, and no valid basis for requiring such segregation can be found in either the Qur'an or the Sunnah. Still, somehow it has become standard practice in mosques throughout the United States and the world outside of Mecca.

This never used to bother me much, as I have always viewed the construction of physical spaces solely for the purpose of worship to be inherently inconsistent with the full practice of my faith. The greatest acts of faith frequently take place outside of such edifices, and their very existence, in my humble opinion, often has the tendency to restrict faith and practice. My reasoning for never fully considering the importance of mosques has generally been as follows: if God is as close to you as your jugular vein, as the Qur'an clearly states (50:16), then why should we bother building tangible homes for God when we could be building them for the homeless? Surely, they are in greater need of homes than God is, and we would serve Him better by building homes for needy humans than by building them for the omniscient, omnipresent, and incorporeal Almighty. Asra is well aware of this reasoning, but she is also all too aware of the failure of many purportedly religious individuals and institutions to acknowledge the full value of the logical capacities with which God has generously supplied us. As a result, Asra accepts and understands the profound effects that physical constructs can have on metaphysical beliefs.

Asra doesn't choose to sit in the men's section of her mosque because she enjoys it or feels at all welcome or appreciated there. Far from it. She actively chooses to endure the discomfort and nausea associated with sitting there because she is overcome by hope, a hope so determined and unrelenting that it could be the result of nothing short of motherhood. She hopes that if the most prominent physical manifestations of Islam, mosques, begin to more accurately reflect the revelatory essence of Islam, Muslims and non-Muslims will begin to more fully and more accurately understand the faith. She hopes that this improved understanding will lead to greater tolerance. She hopes that greater tolerance will facilitate thought. And ultimately, like every devoted philosopher, teacher, and true believer, she hopes that such thought will in turn expose Truth.

While I pray that one day I will be able to attain the active and tremendous hope that so clearly consumes Asra's day-to-day life, I admit that at present I am less than full of hope. Perhaps this explains the impatience and intolerance that so quickly overwhelmed me during my brief visit to the Morgantown mosque with Asra. With the rest of the very few women attending that Friday service enclosed in the balcony above us, where they had to stand in order to witness the services, I started to feel sick to my stomach. Growing increasingly tired of the booming voice of this supposed imam, and feeling so comfortable with Asra at my side as we whispered and giggled like schoolgirls at the ridiculousness of what this man was preaching, I felt the most at home I ever have inside of a mosque.

After finishing his absurd rant, which appeared to be directed solely at Asra, about how there was no place in Islam for modernization and how there was only one right way to practice, and after long discourses in Arabic to a congregation where less than half of the members actually spoke Arabic, the bellowing cardiologist began talking about how we should tell someone if we see that he is not following the Sunnah correctly. At this point, I blurted, "How do you know that your way is right?" Several men in front of us turned to look at me as the flustered imam responded, "Sister, now is not the time for debate." His response confirmed that I had in fact spoken those words aloud, and not merely silently to myself, as I had originally suspected.

Hearing this misguided man's cop-out response while looking him in the eye, I couldn't believe that people actually trusted *him* to work on their hearts. At the thought of his spreading such hate and misinformation, I began to feel heat rising to my head; I imagine that my face was quickly beginning to match the little red flowers on my chador. Asra turned to me after this verbal exchange to express her encouragement. She informed me that I had just fulfilled her ultimate fantasy. Then, this woman whom I had known for only a few hours proceeded to hug me and tell me that she loved me. The combination of sincere and undue love and hatred in the room soon began to overwhelm me, and I felt the hotness in my head turning to tears. I immediately asked Asra if she minded leaving before the formal prayer began.

She smiled, took my hand, and quietly led me outside, where the rain had since subsided, and where she suggested that we pray at her house. Less than a day after our first face-to-face encounter, Asra had inspired me to speak up where I had never before dreamed possible; she had openly expressed her sincere love for me; she had introduced me to her entire immediate family; and she had welcomed me into her home. She had happily opened the doors of her heart, her home, and her mind to me, and for that, I will be forever changed and grateful.

✦✦✦ ✦✦✦

When I first arrived in West Virginia, after a ten-hour drive from Atlanta to Morgantown, I was exhausted and starving. I met Asra at Café of India, in downtown Morgantown, home of West Virginia University (WVU) and, as far as I could gather, not much else. She called me soon after I arrived and asked me if I would be fine with doing the interview at her house. I happily agreed, put in a takeout order, and sat down on an enormous elaborately carved wooden bench at the front of the restaurant, waiting for her to arrive.

She came to meet me at the restaurant so that I could follow her home because, as a hometown girl who had lived in Morgantown since the age of ten, she appeared to have difficulty with street names, being so overwhelmed with the landmarks of her own life permeating this small town. The second Asra walked into the restaurant, I immediately recognized her from the cover of her book. Only weeks before, after requesting an interview through her publicist, I had received a package in the mail from HarperSanFrancisco, including a letter accepting my request; a complimentary copy of Asra's latest book, *Standing Alone in Mecca*; and copies of several news clippings about her efforts to reclaim women's spaces in mosques and Islamic communities around the United States.

I was astonished that Asra, an accomplished author and reporter for the *Wall Street Journal* for over a decade, was willing to let me, an absolute rookie and total stranger, do an interview, when she was simultaneously receiving requests from the likes of the *New York Times*, the *Washington Post*, and other renowned media outlets. I read Asra's book in one sitting, and I only had to read the first five pages to realize that Asra and I were indeed on the same page. "From my earliest days," she writes, "I had been a person on pilgrimage."[1] In my copy of the book, an enormous smiley-face appears next to this sentence, the first of many. Little did I know when I was drawing all of those smiley faces that not only had I found an author with a common dream and purpose but that I had also found a woman who would eventually become a great teacher and friend.

〃〃 ＼＼＼

Asra was born in Bombay, India, in 1965. At the age of four, she moved with her family to the U.S. They first lived in Piscataway, New Jersey, where her father, Zafar, was earning his Ph.D. in nutrition from Rutgers. The family moved to Morgantown when she was ten. There, her father began teaching as an assistant professor of nutrition at WVU, and her mother, Sajida, opened a boutique, Ain's International, which sold largely Indian imports. Asra grew up, like many first-generation Americans, faced with an ever-present identity crisis: too American to be considered fully Indian, and too Indian to be considered fully American. She writes: "As I entered adulthood, I began confronting the boundaries in my life, accepting them at times and daring to challenge them at other times. My father had his own struggles reconciling his culture with his beliefs, but as a scientist he firmly believed in having an open mind and pursuing intellectual inquiry, and he encouraged me to develop these attributes. My father crossed state borders to drive me to New York City so that I could do a summer internship at *Harper's* magazine, but he was also crossing a much more profound kind of line: the cultural tradition that a daughter didn't leave her father's home except to go to her husband's house."[2]

Asra earned her bachelor's degree in liberal arts from WVU in 1986 and went on to earn a master's degree in international communications from American University in 1990. She began working as a staff writer for the *Wall Street Journal* in 1988, and she published her first book, *Tantrika: Traveling the Road of Divine Love*—a memoir about her research of the Tantra tradition, which began as a *Journal* assignment—in 2004.[3] After having spent twelve years at the *Journal*, she is now a full-time freelancer engaged in the seemingly endless process of remodeling her home. Asra moved into the house she grew up in and loves the idea of being able to raise her own son there, with her parents living less than a mile away. Asra's two-year-old son, Shibli, is absolutely adorable, and I bonded with him immediately, as he is outgoing, friendly, talkative, and bears a striking resemblance to my nephew Cyrus.

Shibli's name means "lion cub" in Arabic, and Asra could not have picked a more suitable name for him. He is curious, confident, and adventuresome. Strapping him into the leopard-print car seat in the back of her Suzuki SUV, Asra begins waiving her arms and singing, "Shibli and Mommy on an adventure, Shibli and Mommy on an adventure." Shibli is bouncing in his car seat, flailing his limbs and singing along, as Asra turns to me and revises what is plainly a favorite song of theirs. Shibli quickly chimes in: "Shibli and Mommy and Auntie on an adventure, Shibli and Mommy and Auntie on an adventure." Shibli is indeed no stranger to adventure. His middle name is Daneel, and his namesake was no ordinary man.

Asra gave Shibli this name in homage to Daniel Pearl, a friend of nearly ten years with whom she had worked at the *Journal*. Asra was living in Pakistan and trying to organize her pilgrimage to Mecca when Danny and his pregnant wife, Mariane, arrived in Pakistan. They had found out only a day before their arrival that they were having a baby boy. The next day, January 23, 2002, Danny left Asra, Mariane, and his unborn son, as he had landed what he thought was an investigative interview with a man who was alleged to have had ties with Richard Reid, the clumsy and notorious "shoe-bomber." After five subsequent agonizing weeks of searching for Danny, the world witnessed his videotaped murder at the hands of "Muslim" extremists, who had brutally tortured and murdered him, apparently for no other reason than his being a Jew. Asra writes:

> In the name of my religion, men had slaughtered Danny, a young man with dreams no more complicated than to buy a double bass for his fortieth birthday, love his wife, parents, and sisters, and nurture his son.
>
> Instead of Danny's dreams being realized, police were interrogating four young men who were charged with plotting Danny's kidnapping. They considered themselves devout Muslims. While planning Danny's kidnapping, they had interrupted their strategy sessions to bow their heads toward Mecca for the obligatory five-times-a-day prayers. His murderers videotaped Danny talking about his Jewish heritage, which, in their puritanical Muslim hatred of Jews, was enough to sentence him to death. Among Danny's last words were: "I am a Jew." To my shock, Danny's murderers slandered the name of Islam by killing in its name.
>
> On the dawn after the news of Danny's murder, I was standing in the abyss of darkness wrought by man's distortion of religion. I was engulfed in a pain that made me feel the angels cry when it rained that morning. I was angry. I was afraid. I was sick to my stomach when I even dared to allow myself to feel. Yet, in the sacred space of my womb, life had been created.[4]

Shibli grew as his mother was enduring this great trauma, loss, and torment, and it was he who finally brought her solace. While in Pakistan, Asra had been dating a Pakistani man with whom she had fallen in love and discussed future plans for marriage. She remembers, "He told a friend, yelling into his cell phone as we entered an elevator at the Karachi Sheraton Hotel and Towers, 'I've met the woman I'm going to marry!'"[5] Only two days after Danny's disappearance, however, this man came to see Asra, telling her that Pakistani intelligence officers had questioned him, his family, and his friends in order to discover what they knew about Danny and Asra. His heart was so overcome by fear, apparently, that love no longer had a chance.

After that visit, he stopped coming to see Asra, who was understandably heartbroken. Only three weeks after Danny's disappearance, Asra discovered that she was pregnant. She called the unknowing father and asked him to come see her. When he came, she told him that she was carrying his child, and after a deep breath, he said, "I have to go."[6] For the strong, love acts as a powerful anti-dote to fear, but for the weak, love often disintegrates in the face of fear. Asra writes of her son: "He lived because I had chosen life over fear. He smiled because I had chosen happiness over shame. He grew because I believed the present and the future define us, not the past. He was the result of my efforts to be a better person, to flow toward the divine."[7]

Shibli was only a few months old when he joined his mother on their first pilgrimage to Mecca for Hajj. Asra felt strongly that Shibli should come on this pilgrimage with her because it was he who had been responsible for her reentry into the heart of Islam. Still, bringing Shibli with her made her a crimi-nal under Saudi Arabian law. Her crime? Bearing a child out of wedlock. The evidence against her? Her own angelic son. She refused, however, to let this interfere with Shibli's right to experience his own power and Source.

The dawn of Islam commenced with a slave woman, Hajar, who gave birth to Ishmael. His father, Abraham, had taken Hajar as a second wife because his first wife, Sarah, was unable to bear children. Eventually, Sarah did give birth to Isaac after Ishmael was born, and so follow the Judeo-Christian traditions. Ishmael and Hajar, however, are often forgotten figures in history, even Islamic history. Still, there is no denying they are at its source. The story continues with Sarah eventually growing resentful of Hajar and demanding that Abraham send her and Ishmael into the desert. Abraham did so, on orders from God in a test of his faith, taking them to the middle of a dry, barren desert in the valley of Mecca. He left them alone in the desert with only a bag of dates and a small supply of water. When Hajar asked Abraham why he was abandoning them thus, she discovered that he had been ordered to do so by God. She accepted her fate.

After her abandonment, Hajar continued to breastfeed her son, drink-ing what little water Abraham had left them, but soon both the water and her milk dried up. Ishmael began to cry, and in her desperation, Hajar ran between the hills of Safa and Marwah seven times in search of water. Before she could begin her eighth trip, however, she collapsed from despair and exhaustion next to her crying son. Ishmael was kicking the ground in his fit of tears when water began to spring from the spot where his heel had touched the earth. This is believed to have been the work of the angel Gabriel, and the spring still exists today: the well of *zamzam*. Like many Muslims, I store a little *zamzam* water (the most recent installment being a gift from my cousin from her last pil-grimage) in the fridge for spiritual emergencies.

There is a common impression—some would say superstition—that imbibing water from the well of *zamzam* carries with it a distinctive bestowal of strength and acuity. I'm not above drinking a little bit now and then before an exam, or a long journey, or a particularly important or difficult event. The water is said to quench both thirst and hunger, and part of the pilgrimage requires following in the footsteps of Hajar and drinking from the well of *zamzam*. The origins of Islam thus date back to this frantically desperate mother and slave and her abandoned "bastard" son. Islam is a religion that grew from the victory of righteousness over oppression, and Hajar's story is no exception. While her struggles are often overlooked in religious and scholarly studies of Islam, these struggles in fact mark the birth of this great faith, and until we recognize Hajar's sufferings as our own, we will never be able to fully appreciate and embrace ourselves as Muslims.

Asra recognizes this struggle all too personally. She was still breastfeeding when she went on the Hajj in February 2003. She recounts:

> As Shibli suckled, the sounds of the morning call to prayer erupted into the cool air and reverberated in his ears. It was the same azan, the same call to prayer, that my father had whispered into his ear at his birth. In the holiest place for Muslims, Shibli was hearing the call from the muezzin, the person who makes the call to prayer, of Mecca. There is only one line added to the morning azan: "Prayer is better than sleep."
>
> That moment meant so much to me. I was in Mecca, a criminal in this land for having given birth without a wedding ring on my finger. And I was nursing my son at the holy mosque of Mecca, overlooking the sacred Ka'bah. This was nature's law expressing itself, more powerfully than man's law. I drank the sacred water called zamzam. From me, it flowed into Shibli. I recognized then the great lineage I had in Islam. I was a daughter of Hajar. I looked up to the sky with one thought: blessed are the daughters of Hajar.[8]

When Shibli was born, Asra actively and thoughtfully chose to raise her son as a Muslim. She chose not to let the lies and aggressions of others prevent her son from experiencing his birthright and the true beauty of Islam. She chose not to let anyone make her feel ashamed of that which she was in fact most proud. She chose, no matter how unpopular it made her, to live her life honestly, openly, and responsibly. I can't imagine setting a better example for all of our children, and with such examples speaking up and encouraging the rest of us to do the same, I can easily see Asra's hope becoming just as contagious as her courage. And while my hope for the future of Islam grows in the presence of Asra, it absolutely balloons in the presence of Shibli.

The night I was leaving Morgantown, Asra was scheduled to be on ABC's *Nightline*. She was nervous because she didn't know how the other commentator, Reza Aslan, a young scholar and the author of the book *No god but God*, would comment. She told me that he was an Iranian Shi'ite like myself, and I immediately began praying that he wouldn't make the rest of us look bad. We went to Asra's parents' house to watch the program with her mother, father, and Shibli. Her father was setting up what seemed like every VCR in the house to record the segment. The piece focused on Asra's struggles with the local Morgantown mosque: her insistence on walking through the mosque's front door, as opposed to the back door, where women are "supposed" to enter; her refusal to leave the mosque when the men continuously ask her to; her insistence on her right to pray in her hometown mosque as an equal before God; and her unrelenting conviction that she will not allow misdirected, misogynistic men and women to distort and define her faith for her or for the rest of the world.

Several members of the mosque, who were far from supportive of Asra's efforts, were also interviewed. A man with an overgrown beard, an accent, and a little crocheted hat similar to those worn by some Muslim men had been chosen to speak for the lot. He was not the cardiologist, but he had just as little sense. After he finished his tirade, the show went to commercial, and Shibli turned to his mother: "What was he saying?" Asra told him that the man was talking about how women should have their place. Shibli immediately cut her off midsentence. "NO!" he roared assuredly, as one would expect from a lion cub. I was amazed at the quickness of Shibli's bullshit detector. While he is a highly precocious child, this gut reaction stemmed from more than mere precocity; it was full of the natural unadulterated common sense that so often accompanies instinct. If only grown-ups could have that much sense about them.

After the first set of commercials ended, the program soon focused on Reza Aslan's response, and I grew increasingly nervous, hoping this man would get it. Thank God, he did. In response to questions about men and women praying side by side, he said only that if it was good enough for the Prophet (which it clearly was), then it should be good enough for us. When the piece was over, happiness and relief filled the room, where there had been only hope and anxiety before. "We did it! We won! We did good!" Asra kept saying in varying combinations. Nowhere in all of this excitement did I once hear her use the word "I."

Asra had told me in the car on the way over to her parents' house that she was sure that we would win, that sense and knowledge would prevail over inane traditions and hierarchies to define Islam for the world. When I asked her how she could be so sure, her response was easy: "We're smarter than they are."

This immediately made me think of Molham, and all of Asra's allies, largely unknown to her. Listening to her reminder that we are smarter than the demagogues, I could hear Molham's words repeating in my head: "I have this theory that the ideas that are better win—eventually at least, and this country is all about encouraging the best ideas." I don't think Asra or Molham would disagree that sometimes the best ideas are also the most unpopular, but neither Asra nor Molham is the kind of person to let that fact prevent the personal pursuit or advocacy of those ideas.

A few hours before the *Nightline* special aired, Asra told me that a lot of the people who had been supportive when she was writing the book had since become less so, claiming that she was merely a publicity monger. What was most amusing about this for me was the fact that many of these people had not expressed their objections to her face, but rather through the media. Besides that, such detractors also managed to ignore the fact that, given the opportunity, Asra has an obvious and consistent tendency to promote others in lieu of herself.

For example, she arranged a historic woman-led prayer in New York on March 18, 2005, which was covered all over the national and international media. Asra, however, did not lead the prayer, though she had organized and publicized it. Instead, she asked a scholar by the name of Amina Wadud to lead the prayer. Despite this fact, however, or the fact that she consistently speaks out in support of the struggle for women's rightful place within the practice of Islam without mentioning the name of her book or asking anyone to buy it, many have still chosen to condemn and criticize her as a shameless publicity seeker or self-promoter.

Whatever publicity Asra is seeking, she is seeking it to improve popular perceptions and understandings of Islam. By exposing the failings of a small minority of greatly mistaken, though highly vocal, self-proclaimed Muslims to comply with Islam's unmistakable demands for the equal treatment of women, men, and non-Muslims, Asra is giving other Muslims the courage to restore and reclaim Islam as the logical and glorious spiritual path that it is. She is reminding us that Islam is a faith based in reason, equality, and justice and that hatred and bigotry have no proper place in any true Islamic practice.

Much of the problem with the institutionalization and perception of Islam today comes down to communications and public relations, and the most rational and efficient way to address such a problem is through education and exposure. Faced with a public relations problem, in other words, it only makes sense to engage and educate the public, and it's no secret that Islam faces a serious public relations crisis in the West. Resolving this crisis, as with any other PR crisis, will require a PR response, engaging and educating the public. Such a response, by its very nature, doesn't promote individuals. It promotes ideas and learning, and it can't be achieved quietly. Asra is committed to educating and empowering women in and through Islam, as well as promoting the recollection and practice of the faith's most basic, fundamental, and original precepts. Where and when publicity can help her do this, Asra is not shy about receiving it. That's not self-promotion. That's common sense.

⁄⁄⁄ ⟩⟩⟩

I led a prayer for the first time in my life in Asra's backyard, with only Asra and Shibli following along at my side. We prayed on a colorful patchwork quilt that her mother had made, and she loaned me a pretty pink scarf for the occasion. Asra insisted that I lead the prayer, despite my open declaration that I was sure that my words and technique would somewhat deviate from what she was used to, given the fact that I had learned to pray Shi'a style and that I generally recited a small portion of my prayers in Farsi. By insisting that I lead the prayer regardless, Asra opened the doors of possibility for me. She unknowingly gave me a certain permission, which I never knew I needed or wanted, to be more fully myself.

Reading *Standing Alone in Mecca*, I first learned the meaning of my last name: it's a derivation of the Arabic term *muezzin*, meaning the one who recites the call to prayer. Meeting Asra, I had the great and unexpected surprise of discovering that I could actually live up to that name. Through her simple invitation, Asra gave me the permission, which I had so unknowingly needed, to embrace the full history and capacity of my faith and my family. Asra claims that, through her activism, she is working to find *her* rightful place in Islam. This claim, however, is somewhat deceiving, and by now, I know Asra well enough to know this and assuredly say so. If she were simply looking to find her own proper personal place in the faith, she would have been a hell of a lot quicker and quieter about it. But she wasn't.

If Asra intends to achieve exclusively personal benefits from her activism, she's being incredibly dumb about it, and Asra is no dummy. The aims of her activism are clearly much bigger and broader than herself, and Asra's outspoken statements and actions along these lines have consistently served to elicit nasty and disturbing threats against her life and person. Still, she remains undeterred. Asra values honesty above security, love above hate, justice above vengeance, peace above war, and hope above fear. Not only have these values allowed her to look outside of and past herself (something humans are generally pretty unlikely and reluctant to do), but they have also managed to do much more than that. They have compelled her to *act* on her vision, even in the face of extreme and extensive hostility (something humans are generally even more unlikely and reluctant to do). Love her or hate her, Asra is a rare breed by all accounts: a hopeful and determined fighter, fighting the good fight. She is doing it for me, for Molham, for Sarah, for Matthew, for Sanida, for Ameer, for Hafeeza, for Faisal, for Roxana, for Willow. She is doing it for all of us, and I've got to love her for that.

TWELVE

Faisal A.

And the servants of (God)
Most Gracious are those
Who walk on the earth
In humility, and when the ignorant
Address them, they say,
"Peace!"

 —QUR'AN, AL FURQAN (THE CRITERION), 25:63

O ye who believe!
When you go abroad
In the cause of God,
Investigate carefully,
And say not to anyone
Who offers you a salutation:
"Thou art none of a Believer!"

 —QUR'AN, AL NISA (THE WOMEN), 4:94

The issue of Faisal's name caused me way more internal debate than a name ever should. I was sure that he was just as perfect for the book as Faisal R., but I was annoyed by the unavoidable reality that they happened to share the same name. How could I have a table of contents with two Faisals? It would just look so much better if one of them had a different name. But then again, I guess it would just look so much better for a lot of us to go by different names. And I guess that's why some of us do. And the reasons for this are generally better than satisfying some obsessive-compulsive writer looking to create a more aesthetically pleasing table of contents. Although I can't say that other reasons for adopting different names are *all* that much better. Usually, it's just for the convenience of others anyway—mainly, to make it easier for Americans or Egyptians or Zimbabweans to say your name, depending on what country or culture you're in.

People often assume that I'm one of these people, and I tend to take offense at that assumption, not just because it's false but mostly because it implies that I might be somehow trying to hide something about my background or my identity. Not so for me or for anyone else in this book. If there is any one characteristic shared by all of the diverse individuals profiled here, it has to be that not a single one of us is ashamed or afraid or even just annoyed at the prospect of being him- or herself. None of us has picked a more socially or culturally acceptable name. No matter what society or culture we find ourselves in, we aren't about to change our names or our selves for mere convenience. In this respect, we are all take-it-or-leave-it propositions: we're not going to adjust or modify ourselves for acceptance. We've all, through completely different paths, come to at least one identical conclusion: we'd rather others hate us, than hate ourselves. And as it turns out, I've found that when you don't care what others think, when you follow your heart no matter what the rest of the world is telling you, when you don't bother trying to fit in, when you save your energy and just tell the truth, you're much easier to get along with anyway.

So there was no way I could expect either one of my Faisals to go by a different name. Their refusal to do something like this was exactly what had attracted me to them in the first place. Having realized early on that I was compiling more questions than answers in the process of writing this book, I knew better than to expect that there would be some neat and easy way to tie everything up with a simple and symmetrical bow. Some way so that no people so different from each other could have the same name, some way so that no one might get offended, some way so that everyone would understand, and some way so that everything would make perfect sense. I knew much better than to expect something like that. Of course, there would be no neat and tidy ending, or categories, or table of contents. Life just doesn't work that way. That's what fiction is for.

Just as two highly different individuals can easily share the same name, many highly different individuals can and do call themselves Muslim, and that means a great many different things to a great many different people. For Faisal A., otherwise known as Faisal Alam, being Muslim means facing the truth no matter how messy that promises to be. It means taking on a burden that others are too weak or afraid to bear, speaking out when others are too shy or nervous to speak, and graciously accepting and embracing unpopularity in exchange for honesty and humanity.

I first found out about Faisal when Asra was coming to Atlanta last year as a keynote speaker at the annual Al-Fatiha conference. She asked me to come meet her at the Holiday Inn where the conference was being held, and I agreed, excited just to see her. I was clueless about Al-Fatiha. I knew it was the opening verse of the Qur'an, but I had never heard of any group by that name. So I looked it up online and quickly found out that the Al-Fatiha Foundation is a nonprofit organization devoted to GLBTIQ Muslims, with chapters all over the world.*

I also quickly found out that the group had had a fatwa issued against them in 2001 by Al-Muhajiroun, some international fundamentalist "Islamic" organization with the stated expansive and impossible goal of establishing a global Islamic caliphate.[1] Al-Muhajiroun made headlines for its conference "The Magnificent 19," praising the terrorist attacks of September 11, 2001.[2] Ironically, the name "Al-Muhajiroun" means "The Emigrants" in Arabic, for in August 2005, the group's leader, Omar Bakri Muhammad, was understandably banned from the UK by Home Secretary Charles Clarke because his presence was not "conducive to the [British] public good."[3] His presence is even less conducive to the *Islamic* public good, as promoting criminal acts of violence and murder is antithetical to the most basic Islamic notions of peace, justice, and equality. The fatwa against Al-Fatiha called all of its members apostates and condemned all of them to death.[4]

Faisal Alam founded Al-Fatiha in 1998 (when he was only nineteen years

---

*"GLBTIQ" refers to gay, lesbian, bisexual, transgender, and intersex individuals, as well as individuals questioning their sexuality.

Faisal A.

old), and from what I could ascertain, he had been the recipient of more than his fair share of personal death threats as a result. Thus, understandably, to gain entrance to the group's conference, I had to call and speak with Faisal first: a sort of screening process, mostly for safety purposes. When I told him that I was a friend of Asra Nomani's and that she had invited me, however, Faisal immediately let down his guard and said that of course I was welcome. I then thanked him and told him that I respected and appreciated what he was doing and couldn't wait to meet him.

When I met Asra in the hotel lobby, she was still working on her speech. In fact, I don't think she'd even written anything down yet, and she was scheduled to speak in less than an hour. I wasn't worried for her, though. She's the kind of person who speaks better off the cuff than most people speak after hours of tedious preparation. And indeed, as I expected, she gave a fabulous speech, received a standing ovation, and came back down into the crowd to take her seat next to me, yet again making me proud as hell to be sitting beside her.

Afterward, people started approaching her in flocks, and I tried to get away to leave her to her admiring public, but she squeezed my arm, pulling me back beside her, insisting on introducing me to everyone and anyone. Asra's not an easy person to desert. She told me to come back over the next two days for the workshops, and I accepted the invitation. I hadn't paid a registration fee—or even registered, for that matter—but she said not to worry about it.

When I came back, I came with Matthew, who seemed even more excited about the conference than I did. At the closing dinner, Asra, Matthew, and I were all unknowingly sitting around the same table as Sarah's father, who had come to the conference (like the rest of us) as an "ally," and whom Asra and I had dubbed the Ralph Nader of Muslim America because of his extensive knowledge of very specific facts and his history as an activist. When he told us that he had spent time in a Sudanese torture house, I probably should have put two and two together, but it wasn't until months later that it hit me and that Sarah confirmed that her dad was indeed our knowledgeable and beloved table companion on that particular evening. Finding this out somehow made me feel like I was on the right track. There just seemed to be too many coincidences tying everyone together, and I've never been a believer in "coincidence" as anything short of divine intervention.

The problem with reading signs into everything, however, is that, for me at least, the signs seem to always be pushing me into even deeper trouble and requiring more work. Sometimes it's just easier to ignore them, but I'd rather be in a lot more trouble, with a lot more work to do, than lose my path altogether. So I give myself up to the direction of the signs more often than not, and I think that much of the genuine self-respect that I have managed to gather in my short life is due entirely to this abdication.

I don't remember many of the details about the Al-Fatiha workshops, but I do remember Faisal. He seemed to be running *everything*. He spoke at the closing dinner, affirming that he would be stepping down as the volunteer director and the president of the board of directors in order to further pursue his education, but noting that he would still be involved. Honestly, I don't know if he actually did step down, though. If he did, it would be hard to tell because he's still doing so much work for and with Al-Fatiha.

What struck me most and most immediately about Faisal was his face. He had this sort of perma-smile, which didn't appear to be even the least bit strained. It was the kind of face that made you want to come up to him, kiss both cheeks, and introduce yourself. From the warmth and openness emanating from his face alone, you'd think that he didn't have a trouble in the world. But looks can be deceiving.

In addition to Faisal, Amina Wadud was also scheduled to speak that evening. In the middle of her speech, however, a young black woman in full *hijab* literally *burst* into the room. I can't remember her exact words, but her hateful intentions were clear. She said something along the lines of *How dare you call yourselves Muslims!* She was sufficiently booed and left as quickly as she came, but not before the resident imam—the distinguished and both physically and intellectually formidable Imam Daayiee Abdullah, hitherto completely sweet and cool tempered—ran after her. All I could hear from inside the ballroom was Daayiee saying, "How dare *you*!" The next thing I knew, Dr. Wadud was asking us not to let this interruption faze us. We all tried to bring ourselves back, but for me, at least, it was impossible to hear a single word she said after that.

All I could think about was how proud I was to be part of this group and how this was the first time in my life that I really felt welcome as a Muslim for who I was. No modifications necessary. For the first time ever in a group of Muslims, I didn't feel the need to censor my body or my soul. On top of that, I felt safe, protected, and understood. I trusted Brother Daayiee to say and do all that needed to be said and done—ten times better than I could have ever attempted. It felt so odd and refreshing to be able to relax for once and know that *I* didn't have to deal with all that ugly, hateful bullshit. Brother

Faisal A.

Daayiee, a trained and respected Islamic scholar, had *my* back. I will always love him for doing what he did that day. If I never see him again in my life, he will always hold a place in my heart and in my prayers.

/// \\\

I kept Faisal's number, and after the conference I began courting him like a desperate and rapidly aging spinster. I just had to know who this guy was. He had to be more than an agenda, but in article after article that I read about him, that's all I saw him portrayed as: this living, breathing, walking agenda. But that's just not who he is. Who-he-is is so much more complicated, but that doesn't make for good headlines. It honestly takes spending just a few minutes alone with him to realize that Faisal is way more than some specific agenda, but it seems like that's a few more minutes than most of the reporters interviewing him had to spare.

He is, in fact, a unique and complicated human being. But he has done this *huge* thing (essentially founding the world's largest Muslim GLBTIQ organization), and as such, it is supremely easy to reduce Faisal to his accomplishments—because they are just so many and so massive. I have zero doubt that by creating Al-Fatiha, Faisal has literally saved hundreds of lives at least. Suicide is perhaps *the* leading cause of death among gay and lesbian youth today, and GLBTIQ Muslims are far from immune to the truth behind these statistics; if anything, they are even more affected than their non-religiously affiliated counterparts.[5] Upon discerning that they do not easily fit into the "normal" or "acceptable" world of heterosexuality, many GLBTIQ Muslims seriously consider suicide. It is my sincere belief, moreover, that the simple fact that Al-Fatiha exists has dissuaded more than a few such suicides.

So today, when I hear people spewing ignorant blanket statements regarding Islam and homosexuality ("Islam forbids homosexuality," or "A homosexual *cannot* be Muslim"), I immediately wonder how many lives *those* people have managed to save in between making their automatic and idiotic proclamations. I think one would be hard pressed to find a Muslim, a Christian, or a Jew who does not accept the original Talmudic teaching, reaffirmed in the Holy Qur'an, that one who saves a single life, saves the world entire.* Yet people can be so quick to take on the crass and inhuman business of judging

---

*The Talmudic cites for this are Sanhedrin 4:1 (22a) and Sanhedrin 37a. The Qur'anic cite is 5:32: "And if anyone saved a life / It would be as if he saved / The life of the whole people."

Faisal A.

and damning that they often end up overlooking humanity entirely. It is a basic teaching of Islam, Christianity, and Judaism that only God is fit to judge us, but somehow this teaching has escaped the minds of so many Muslims, Christians, and Jews, especially when it comes to issues relating to sexuality. It would do us all some good to suspend judgments that we are not equipped, experienced, or qualified to make.

⟋⟍ ⟍⟍

See! There I go: doing exactly what I maligned all those other writers for doing when reporting on Mr. Faisal Alam: turning him into an *agenda*. Like I said, it's hard not to do it, given everything this young man has achieved. Nevertheless, I consider myself at a decided advantage in "reporting" on Faisal because I have had the privilege of his friendship. As a friend, I can't ignore the fact that Faisal is a serious activist at heart; that he has a penchant for the overlooked, the marginalized, and the oppressed; and that all of his e-mails end with the following quote from Mahatma Gandhi: "Be the change you want to see in the world." Across the board, Faisal is not the kind of guy who can just sit back and do nothing when he sees something awry. He'll fix your collar if it's uneven; he'll tuck in the tag on the back of your shirt if it's sticking out; and he'll tell you if you have broccoli in your teeth or ketchup on your face.

When I finally sat down to interview Faisal, almost a year after he said he'd let me, we were already friends, and so, I knew he would be late. We met at a local coffee shop on a sunny Sunday morning in late October. He was actually doing quite well at being on time—only fifteen minutes late. But as always, he was overly apologetic. His exact first words were, "I'm not even awake yet. I'm so sorry. I'm so sorry." I gave him permission to get some coffee, and when he was fully assured that I didn't want any, he walked over to the cashier. When he got back, I handed him a bag full of some Persian food that I had cooked the night before. He was just as overly grateful when I handed it to him as he was overly apologetic when he first walked in.

I was set up in a corner of the café next to an outlet, with my computer plugged in and my recorder at the ready. When he sat down, Faisal said we could go outside if I wanted because the music was so loud. I told him not to fret, that I would ask them to turn it down. A look of shock overtook his ridiculously kind face: "You're not *really* going to *do* that?" I assured him it was no big deal, though he didn't believe me, and when I came back and told him that the cashier had thanked me because he hated the music and would gladly turn it down, Faisal seemed surprised and impressed. He doesn't like to inconvenience people and will avoid doing so as much as humanly possible. He's always more concerned about the comfort of others than he is about his own.

Oddly enough, I sensed some discomfort on his part once we got settled into our little corner. I was supremely comfortable—dressed in nothing but soft cotton layers with no zippers to speak of, unshod, legs curled up under me. Faisal, however, didn't seem to be himself entirely, and I think he sensed that I noticed this because he kept talking about how sleepy he was. It didn't take long for me to recognize the source of his discomfort.

Faisal is incredibly wary of journalists and reporters—and for good reason: he was outed by the *New York Times* in 1999, in a small article in the B section that got picked up by members of his Muslim community, including his family, in Connecticut. Then in 2000, another piece appeared in the *Washington Post* that was syndicated in at least four major newspapers across the country. The *Post* article included a photo of Faisal, and after that, he was *way* out, whether he wanted to be or not. He missed the chance to come out privately to his family, all because of some eager, ambitious, and absentminded journalist. I understand his caution. But while Faisal was completely unconcerned about anything having to do with *him* personally, when it came to other people in his life (his family, his ex-fiancé, his friends), he was exceedingly cautious. He didn't want to inadvertently spit something out that could potentially hurt anyone else in any way, and even though I assured him that I would not publish anything he was uncomfortable with, and would let him review his chapter before signing his release, he was still super-tentative. He had learned his lesson about writers, and friend or not, he wasn't going to make the same mistake again.

Thus, Faisal spent over four hours telling me the story of his life that morning, making sure the whole time not to reveal most anyone's real name.. His speech was painfully full of pseudonyms. He was constantly censoring people, names, and events to protect *someone else*. I'd never seen him so careful with his words before. I can't imagine how exhausting four hours of such intense self-monitoring could be, but he seemed unfazed. I then realized how incredibly routine this whole scenario must be for him, and for the first time, I recognized what a truly heavy burden he was carrying behind that warm and placid face of his.

>>> <<<

Faisal A.

Faisal grew up in Germany, Saudi Arabia, Pakistan, and Connecticut, respectively. His father was a civil engineer in the U.S. Army Corps of Engineers, which was largely responsible for his somewhat nomadic childhood. Born in Frankfurt to Pakistani immigrants, he spoke German as his first language, and he spent the first six years of his life in Germany. He spent the next four years in Saudi Arabia, where he went to an international British school, learning English and forgetting German. Then he spent several months in Pakistan, and after that, at the age of ten, he and his family moved to Ellington, Connecticut (human population roughly fourteen thousand).[6] "We used to call it Smellington," Faisal boasts sarcastically, "because it had more cows than people."

Concerning his parents' marriage, Faisal uses the phrase "shotgun wedding," which of course makes me think that his mother was pregnant when his parents got married. So I ask him to clarify, and he replies, "Oh, that's what 'shotgun wedding' means? Then no . . . it was just quick, within a week. I don't understand these American idioms. I swear to God! And I tell people: look, any cultural references before 1987—I'm not going to understand. I mean, people say all these things, and I'm like, huh? What? Who's *Mork and Mindy?* And I'm like, listen, I know everything from *Punky Brewster* forward. That's it." It's odd to hear that he has trouble with American idioms and pre-1987 cultural references because he just sounds and looks so damn American. He has no accent; he's always hip and stylish in his dress and demeanor. I just figured that he was this guru of pop culture—past and present—but apparently there is this big gap in his experience about which I had no idea.

He describes his parents as "polar opposites." His mom is a do-gooder type who teaches special education, when she isn't teaching immigrant women how to drive and speak English. His dad now works for the State Department and travels a lot. He seems to have been more of the disciplinarian, and by Faisal's account, he is quick-tempered and petulant. They divorced not long ago, but Faisal says that they never really got along.

Faisal, who grew up attending mosque, says that the mosque his family attended in Connecticut split three times that he can remember because of various ideological differences. He remembers one day when his family came to the mosque to find that a new partition had been put up between the men and the women. Apparently, by the end of the prayer, his mother had torn down the partition entirely. The next week's entire sermon was about the dangers of improperly dressed and improperly behaving women. At the end of that sermon, according to Faisal, the women were all out in the parking lot yelling at their husbands for letting the imam get away with all his misguided ranting. Faisal seems to have very clearly inherited his mother's temperament and inclinations: he too began tearing down absurd and unreasonable partitions early in life.

/// \\\

Faisal says that as a child, he hated living in the U.S. because he was in such a small town, one of only five brown kids at his high school (the other four being African American). "My friends at school," he notes, "were always rejects because I was an outsider. . . . I remember one incident when I was a freshman, and this guy who was a junior was walking in the hallway, and he just grabbed me and pushed me, and I fell into, I mean *inside of*, this big green plastic dumpster. And he told me, 'Go back to your country.' He got in a lot of trouble after that, though, and he never looked at me again. . . . But I grew up with kids making fun of me, saying stupid things like, 'Where's your flying carpet?' or 'Does your dad work at the 7–11?' or 'Did you bring your camel today?' Stupid stuff like that. I hated it."

Faisal calls himself a 1.5 immigrant, because having come to the U.S. at the age of ten, he's not exactly a first-generation immigrant, but he's not quite a second-generation either. Easily a COFOB, I thought when I heard him tell me this, but I kept the acronym to myself, not wanting to waste time discussing semantics. The semantics were irrelevant—it was the *feel* that mattered. Like many COFOBs, Faisal talks about having a sort of "dual identity": he was going to school every day with American kids and coming home as a "latchkey kid" to watch *Star Trek*, but then again, when his parents got home, the family spoke Urdu and ate Pakistani food.

But Faisal also talks about yet another sort of dual identity, which he says affected his parents more than it did him and his brother. This was the Saturday-night versus Sunday-morning dichotomy. Apparently on a somewhat regular basis, Saturday nights for Faisal's family were characterized by Pakistani parties—his mom would dress up in her finest clothes and wear elaborate jewelry, and they would all go to these parties, and then, "on Sunday, we would wake up and we were Muslim all of a sudden. The jewelry was gone."

"In retrospect," Faisal continues, "God! Talk about living a confusing life." To me, though, it doesn't sound all that confusing. I went to similar parties as a kid and still occasionally attend them even now, with my parents. But we never went to the mosque the next day, and even if we had, I'm pretty sure that the jewelry would still have been there. I guess we all have our own confusing experiences that help mold us into the people we become.

At home and at the mosque, Faisal, growing up, was the picture of a model child. He was religious, spoke Urdu at home, finished his homework, and helped his mother. "I used to love making desserts at all the social functions," he recalls, "and all the aunties used to say that Faisal makes such wonderful desserts, and my mom used to say, 'I don't need a daughter because I have Faisal.'" While he outwardly exuded model behavior, Faisal was concurrently consumed by a deep internal confusion. He was always very interested in his faith, and he began acting upon that interest during his junior year in high school. He started getting very involved in his local Muslim community, organizing youth camps and other events for Muslim youth.

"I was baking desserts and giving speeches at the mosque. I was always wanting to be around the sisters, and all the sisters were always saying how much they loved Brother Faisal. And I wasn't paying attention to the boys at all in a sexual way in the mosque. It was more admiration: wanting to be them, in a way. To play sports, you know, to *be* like them. But I wasn't."

Faisal associates his becoming "really religious" with prom: "You know, it's the point in time when people have to decide if they are going to become Americanized and go to the prom. Are you going to go to the prom or stick to your religious customs?" Actually, I don't know—I'm not quite sure why these two things are necessarily competing interests—but I keep quiet, and Faisal continues. "So, I decided not to go to prom: a decision driven just as much by an increasing awareness of my sexuality as by an aim to please my parents and conform to our cultural norms. I was probably fifteen or sixteen at the time, and I was always opening up different versions of the Qur'an and going to homosexuality in the index; I was reading in the encyclopedia about homosexuality." It was around this same time that Faisal entered into his first romantic relationship.

"I was in a relationship with a guy for about one or two years when I was around sixteen and seventeen. . . . So I was coming to terms with my sexuality while I was also being invited to give presentations about Islam in all the social studies classes at my high school. I had become friends with this white American convert at my mosque. He was ten years older than me. He told me later that he had asked around about me: if I was gay or not. And everyone would say, 'No, Faisal's not gay. He's just religious.'" Turns out Faisal was both: gay *and* religious.

Unfortunately, however, he was living in a world where homosexuality and religion were largely deemed mutually exclusive. I don't pretend that this world is all that different today, but I know for sure that it's changing, and that people like Faisal are leading the way in renovating this warped worldview. Call me an idealist, but I think that, given the chance, most people will choose reason over absurdity, and if anything, Islam encourages its followers to do exactly that. As far as I'm concerned, it is in fact hateful bigotry and faith that are mutually exclusive.

The most basic beliefs across all major religions often turn out looking pretty identical in the end, but people get so caught up in meaningless details that it becomes easy to forget or ignore the key similarities. In no major religion of which I'm aware is hatred for any given group of people necessary or indispensable. I have never seen any harm come from dispensing with hateful beliefs, but I have seen worlds of harm come from espousing them. It is my sincere hope that this valuable lesson will not be lost on my generation, and I take comfort in knowing that Faisal is one of those working hard to guarantee that it isn't.

Faisal began his relationship with the aforementioned unnamed convert he met at the mosque when he was around sixteen years old. "We were both fascinated by Islam. We actually ended up coming out to each other. We were at a Subway [sandwich shop], and we were talking about movie actors. He was saying that he really loved Keanu Reeves, and we were both like, 'Yeah, he's so *hot*.'

"We basically ended up in this relationship. Of course, nobody knew about it. . . . Essentially, we would have these amazing weekends together. . . . But when I would get back home, I would open up every translation of the Qur'an and be on the phone with him crying. He had come out first and *then* converted, so he had a very different experience than I did. . . . I just couldn't figure out why God would create you to hate you. . . . But there was just so much internalized homophobia within myself that I just couldn't deal with it ultimately, and we ended the relationship."

Around the same time, during his senior year in high school, Faisal started becoming very close to a young religious Muslim girl who lived in upstate New York, and they began writing letters to each other. He won't tell me her name, just as he won't tell me his first boyfriend's name. He's hyper-vigilant about respecting everyone's privacy—no matter what the relationship, how it began, or how it ended. He is visibly conscious of the fact that his life is not his own, that it involves and requires other people, and he will go to any lengths to protect their identities. I doubt that many of the people whom he refuses to name would even care if he did so, but he prefers to err on the side of caution. I can't say that I blame him, but I can say that I personally would be offended *not* to be associated with him, given the chance. If, discussing his life with anyone else, Faisal somehow stumbles upon the topic of our friendship, I sincerely hope that he will use my full and exact name and title. Incidentally, I know a good many other people who share my sentiments on this.

At any rate, Faisal continues discussing his relationship with the anonymous girl, ultimately assigning her the pseudonym "Aisha" purely for the sake of convenience. "Our letters were so innocent. They would be like, 'A'salam Alaikum, Brother Faisal. Insha' Allah, all is well with you.' Stuff like that." He's laughing. "On the phone we would talk in third person about our futures, like, 'I want my "husband" to take care of the kids while I go to medical school,' and I would be like, 'I would do that for my "wife."'" It sounds so silly in retrospect, but it was clear that something was there with us. She was very religious— wore *hijab* and everything. . . . All this went on for maybe six or seven months. And then, I remember it was August 24, 1995, and it was a few weeks before I was going off to school in Boston, and I got a phone call from her. She said, 'I don't think we can continue doing this. It's just not right.' I remember I was in the basement of our house, and I said, 'I think I know what you're saying. Will you marry me?' Then there was this long silence on the other end—she was very surprised, and she said, 'I can't say no, but I can't say yes.' I said, 'I understand.' Essentially, two weeks later, she called and said yes on the phone, and she said, 'You need to talk to your parents, and they should talk to my parents, and you should talk to my dad.'"

Ultimately, none of it worked out, but Faisal still has a very precise memory of the whole experience, or "failed engagement," as he calls it. Her parents were apparently quite keen on the idea of the two marrying, but Faisal's parents were less than enthused. When Faisal finally gathered enough courage to tell his mom that he had asked Aisha to marry him, her first reaction, according to him, was as follows:

"'Why Aisha? She's so plain looking.' She wanted someone to show off with all these fancy jewels and clothes, and because Aisha was so religious and wore *hijab*, that was all sort of out of the question. I said something like, 'You're not going to marry her, I am.' Then she went on about how she would still have to show her off as the bride. . . . And then my mom was like, 'I can get you some girl from Pakistan and throw *hijab* on her if that's what you really want.' And then she went through a list of five other girls we knew who she might have preferred."

His father would have been even more against the idea (if Faisal had ever gathered up the nerve to tell him), as he was beginning to get annoyed by Faisal's heightened religiosity regardless, because he associated being religious with being uneducated. As far as his father was concerned, Faisal was going to college, so that he could go to medical school, so that he could become a doctor, so that he could marry the woman of his father's choosing. Faisal, however, wasn't fitting into any of the molds his family had fashioned for him, and increasingly, he was realizing that he wasn't fitting into the mold he had subconsciously fashioned for himself either.

His communication with Aisha steadily diminished over time because Faisal wasn't able to tell his dad about the engagement, and she understandably wanted things to start moving faster. I find it hard to believe that Faisal was ever afraid to tell anyone anything. The Faisal I know is still very respectful, but he is also strong, brave, confident, and outspoken. As Faisal keeps talking, I begin to realize how incredibly different this handsome young man sitting in front of me is from the boy he is talking about. I'm so strongly struck by this realization that I have to stop listening for a moment, just to fully appreciate the positive and immeasurable evolution of Mr. Faisal Alam.

When I come back from my rumination, Faisal hasn't noticed that I was gone. His capacity for speech is astounding: he's not the kind of person to ever be at a loss for words. He is at that point talking about how Aisha was going to London for this big demonstration in Trafalgar Square during the denouement of their relationship. She was going as part of this group called Hisb ut Tahrir in an effort to convert the entire U.K. to Islam. The sheer ridiculousness of this notion becomes at once comprehensible when Faisal explains that Hisb ut Tahrir is the group from which Al-Muhajiroun (the group that later issued a fatwa against all Al-Fatiha members) had splintered off.

Upon discovering that Aisha would be going on this trip, Faisal sent her these Celtic-looking charms to wear, to keep her safe while she was in Britain. He admits to the absurdity of the gesture and the charms themselves, but he insists that at the time he was very serious about it. She returned the charms in an envelope that apparently also held several strands of her hair—likely unintentionally.

"I was such a romantic at the time," Faisal explains, laughing, "that I put them in an envelope and sealed it, thinking that I would give it to her on her wedding night." He never did. Faisal admits that he was never sexually attracted to Aisha, but he says that he loved her in a platonic and spiritual sense. He appreciated her apparent religiosity, which played a large role in his initial attraction to her.

Faisal is terminally *obsessed* with weddings. "Since I was a kid, I've always fantasized about getting married or having this beautiful, elaborate ceremony. I didn't know who the bride would be or even if there would be a bride. I used to watch Indian movies, and I just loved the wedding scenes. . . . I've always dreamed of having this big wedding." Today, Faisal's fantasies are considerably less realistic, but they are certainly more honest: "I have this fantasy of having this Muslim man, probably Arab or South Asian, who would be dressed in all white, on a white horse, and he would just sweep me off my feet, and I would forever be in love. . . . At one of the Al-Fatiha conferences there was a couple there—one was Malaysian and the other was half Pakistani and half German. . . . It was time to pray, and they came outside and stood next to each other in the prayer, and I just started crying as I saw them start to pray because I thought it was the most beautiful thing in the entire world. They were so at peace with their sexuality and their relationship with God. I remember that night I went up to them at dinner and gave them a rose." Faisal is an incurable romantic, prone to fits of grand delusions. He is a visionary in the truest sense of the word, with an uncanny knack for looking beyond current realities or possibilities.

Aisha broke off her engagement with Faisal in February 1996—over e-mail. He was a freshman at Northeastern University in Boston at the time, and he printed the e-mail out in the computer room and read it while he was walking home, crying the whole way. In August of that same year, she married someone else—"some FOB she met at the mosque." Faisal came out that summer, and he says that for a long time his mom thought that he "became gay" because of the whole failed engagement. Of course, people don't generally just up and "become" gay, any more than they just up and "become" Portuguese. Still, being the incredibly empathetic and protective person he is, Faisal tried his best to reassure his mom that this was indeed not the case.

A year later, Faisal received another e-mail from Aisha, saying that she wanted him to talk to her husband so that he could help Faisal see the error of his ways. He did her the courtesy of calling her, not at all interested in being converted to heterosexuality by Aisha's husband, and as fate would have it, Aisha picked up the phone, and her husband wasn't home. Faisal then told her, "I just want you to know that I didn't become gay because of you. I was always like this, and you didn't do anything wrong." I have absolutely no idea how it is humanly possible to be that supremely courteous, considerate, or forgiving.

I swear, if that moron who issued a fatwa against him somehow magically landed on Faisal's doorstep with a skinned knee, Faisal would probably offer him a Band-Aid and rubbing alcohol without a second thought. I don't know how he does it, but he manages to receive all this hate and yet emit all this love. It's an odd and fascinating thing to witness.

*** ≫≫

Faisal left home when he was eighteen because, he says, he couldn't stand living with his father. He went to Northeastern for a year, until his father stopped paying tuition because Faisal was studying political science instead of medicine. Faisal has just now managed to get around to finishing his last three years of college, attending Atlanta's Georgia Perimeter College on a PFLAG (Parents, Families and Friends of Lesbians and Gays) scholarship. He is also working full-time as an assistant conference planner for a nonprofit organization in Atlanta that works with historically black colleges and universities in order to encourage more minority students to pursue careers in the biomedical and health sciences.

The summer after his first and only year at Northeastern, the summer of 1996, Faisal, in his own words, "exploded out of the closet." Not one to do things halfheartedly, Faisal made it a point to expose himself to every aspect of gay culture in Boston. "For six months," he says, "I was Brother Faisal Alam in the morning, on the board of the Young Muslims of the Islamic Circle of North America (ICNA) and the Northeastern regional representative for the national Muslim Students Association (MSA). In the evening, I was Club-Kid Faisal. . . . I was living a dual life once again. For six months that went on, but then in November I had a nervous breakdown. I went back to Connecticut, and I was in the hospital for two weeks. . . . The two lives just couldn't continue anymore. I just physically and mentally broke down. The whole world was calling and wondering what had gone wrong, so it was at that time in the hospital when I decided that I needed to bring these two parts of my life back together."

I imagine it's not easy to reach such sound and rational conclusions at the tail end of a nervous breakdown, but Faisal works well under pressure. Most people in Faisal's position would probably have had a nervous breakdown years earlier, and most people quite possibly could have been debilitated for life. But Faisal's a fighter—and not in any ordinary sense of the word.

People are forever making "heroes" out of the sick and the ailing. I know, having been one of them for quite some time. I call it the Christopher Reeves Syndrome, and I feel like the whole world has it. When I was sick, people were always telling me what a great "fight" I was putting up and how "strong" I was being. But the truth is, I had no other option—unless one considers suicide a viable option. I just hung out and let the doctors do the best they could. There's nothing "heroic" about that. Just like there's nothing heroic about searching for the cure for a disease from which you yourself are suffering. That's called self-preservation, and it's basic human instinct.

True heroism requires actions that are not based on self-preservation—actions that will almost inevitably make you unpopular and the object of persecution. True heroism, in this sense, requires opposition. Last I checked, there's no one out there trying to *cause* or increase the incidence of breast cancer or Alzheimer's disease. But there are tons of people out there trying to rid the world of homosexuals and homosexuality. Genuine heroism requires fighting for something besides yourself, knowing that the odds are against you, recognizing the serious risks that such a fight presents to your very person, and then taking on the fight nevertheless. It is in this sense that Faisal is a hero.

He easily could have come to terms with his sexuality and his faith and then shut up about it. But he didn't. He created a refuge for *others* facing similar circumstances, knowing that doing so would garner him hate from all over the world. Faisal started Al-Fatiha as a listserv for gay Muslims, and, he says, he was incredibly naive in doing so—so naive that he didn't think that there would be anyone on the listserv who wasn't *supposed* to be. I don't believe him for a second. He knew he wasn't starting a knitting circle, and he could have stopped at any point, but he didn't.

Al-Fatiha grew into an international phenomenon, was registered as a nonprofit organization, and was holding workshops and conferences all over the place. Something like that just doesn't happen by accident. After starting Al-Fatiha, Faisal was asked to step down from his leadership positions in two separate Muslim organizations: the Young Muslims of the ICNA and the national MSA. If Faisal had had an ounce of self-preservation left in him at that point, he would have given up his efforts entirely, but he didn't. He had a million chances to back out, and, very consistently and determinedly, he not only didn't back out but moved forward. Before Faisal started Al-Fatiha, there was no active international organization for GLBTIQ Muslims. Today there is. Faisal has created a safe space for a huge group of maligned, persecuted, and marginalized individuals. He has done so in the face of fierce hate and opposition, and he has done so under his own name, on his own terms, sacrificing his own time and money. *That's* a hero.

I don't throw that word around lightly or often because it tends to have such inane associations, especially in our modern American culture (think celebrities, debutantes, athletes), but I mean it outside of all these asinine associations. The thing about Faisal is that he couldn't stand being called a hero to his face. His mix of quiet humility, playful sarcasm, and critical wit would find some way around accepting the accurate assessment. And I have to admit that I love that about him. He has achieved more in ten years than most of us will in our entire lifetimes, but he looks down on no one and simply won't let his achievements define him. Rather, he banks largely on his emotions.

Faisal is an extremely emotional person, in that he appears to *feel* certain things more intensely than the rest of us might. It's not just that he can tell when you're uncomfortable, or even that he will go out of his way to comfort you; it's more that he just *bothers*. He's not so consumed with himself that he fails to notice those around him. If you're lucky enough to make his acquaintance, you can be sure that he'll look you in the eye, listen to you, and offer you something or invite you somewhere. I can honestly say that I know no one else quite like him and that I am a better person for knowing him.

Truth Stands out Clear from Error

Let there be no compulsion
In religion: Truth stands out
Clear from Error: whoever
Rejects evil and believes
In God hath grasped
The most trustworthy
Handhold, that never breaks.
And God heareth
And knoweth all things.

—QUR'AN, AL BAQARAH (THE COW), 2:256

When I began writing this book, my aim was simple: to expose the diverse range of Muslim American experiences, while confirming the possibility of being Muslim in America and being American in Islam. In completing this book, however, I find not only that it is *possible* to be both Muslim and American but that, for many people, including myself, this arrangement is in fact ideal. Despite the fact that Muslim Americans are undoubtedly experiencing greater discrimination and persecution today than they did prior to 9–11, and despite the fact that Muslims are increasingly becoming targets of hate crimes, racial profiling, and unlawful arrests throughout the U.S., particularly since passage of the USA PATRIOT Act, America still holds unparalleled opportunities for Muslims and Islam.

As an American of any faith, I can openly comment on the flaws and weaknesses of my government, without fear for my life, my family, or my freedom. Over the summer of 2004, for example, as a lowly second-year law student, I was hired to work with the U.S. Department of Homeland Security for the Congressional Commission on International Religious Freedom to document the treatment of foreign nationals at our borders for the purpose of ultimately improving our nation's treatment of immigrants. As an American, if you're unsatisfied with the system, you can change it: you can vote; you can run for office; you can write a book; you can stage a protest; and most importantly, you can go to school, as long and as far as you like. On top of that, you can count on the great majority of your fellow Americans to be just as curious, freethinking, kind, and open-minded as you are.

Americans have an unmatched penchant for demanding independently verifiable proof. We think for ourselves, and we are highly skeptical. We know when we're being lied to, and we don't take it lightly. The Prophet Muhammad claimed that "the most excellent *jihad* is uttering the truth in the presence of an unjust ruler."[1] In contrast to the faulty notions of *jihad* propagated by sensationalist media sources and foolish fundamentalists, there is no violence involved in this true *jihad*, or struggle: it is at its core the unfettered exercise of free speech. In America, we can fulfill this *jihad* not only by speaking truth to such unjust rulers but also by voting them out. It is the unique American appreciation for skepticism and independent thought that makes this country, in my opinion, the ideal place to begin restoring truth to Islam and the ideal base for the next Islamic Renaissance.

The greatest impediments to this impending Renaissance come from misguided Muslims and misinformed Americans, and the former indisputably fuel the latter. Today, the misguided minorities within Islam—those manipulating the faith to achieve power, wealth, and status; those misreading it to perpetuate their own hatred and ignorance; those maligning it to justify their own violent, murderous actions; and those desecrating it to gain attention and publicity— are gaining the undeserved privilege of defining Islam for the rest of the world simply because they are yelling the loudest and behaving the nastiest.

However, it is up to the majority of us—those who believe that there is only One God and that He is All-Powerful, Merciful, and Compassionate; those who believe that the Qur'an is right to warn us that there should be no compulsion in religion and that Truth stands out clear from error in this world (2:256); and those who know better than to trust our souls in the hands of thieves, liars, and murderers—to speak up, to call the misdirected tiny minority of "Muslims" out on their lies. This miniscule group of highly vocal individuals presents more than just an unfortunate collection of walking public-relations disasters: they are responsible for reinforcing the misinformation of a great many Americans. If we want to educate non-Muslim Americans about the true beauty of Islam, we first have to speak out against this mistaken minority of hate-mongers and power-seekers who fraudulently claim to be acting in the name of Islam.

Our greatest ally in this effort is the Holy Qur'an itself, for when we study the Qur'an, we find that nowhere in this holy text—our only uncontestable source of revelation in Islam—does the Lord teach senseless hate, violence, or coercion. In its prime, Islam was a religion in which rational thought reigned supreme, and with a little hope and foresight, it is not impossible to envision a modern Islamic Renaissance well within our lifetimes.

I will never forget a medieval philosophy course I took during my freshman year at Wesleyan. Taught by the incomparable Stephen Crites, the class took place in a small room in what had been termed the College of Letters, an interdisciplinary department combining the studies of philosophy, history, and literature. The department was separated from the rest of the academic departments on campus and looked like an expansive cottage. It was overrun by trees and other indiscernible foliage, and I remember that it was so much like rats-in-a-maze trying to make it to one of our classroom's bona fide entrances that many of us just chose to climb in through one of the room's many large windows.

One of our first assigned readings for the class was Peter Abelard's *Dialogue of a Philosopher with a Jew and a Christian*. As a budding philosopher, I immediately sided with the Philosopher after reading only a few pages. During our first class discussion of the piece, Professor Crites informed us that there was a widely held view that the Philosopher in the text also, in fact, represented a Muslim. While at the time, I was too uneducated in Islam to understand the great likelihood of this view, or to pick up on the subtle hints in Abelard's text, I was incredibly proud nonetheless. Now, having studied the Qur'an and hadiths as closely as I have Immanuel Kant or Saint Augustine, I more fully comprehend the validity of this view of the Muslim as philosopher, and I speculate that it very well may have been my understated Islamic upbringing that was initially responsible for my intense passion for philosophy. Islam is a faith built upon reason, education, and a sincere recognition of human nature.

If anyone is to rescue Islam from the distortions and manipulations to which a small number of misinformed fanatics are subjecting it, it will be the logical, freethinking, and outspoken Muslims of the world. More than anything, at this point in time, Islam is in desperate need of critical and rational thinkers. Such thinkers are emerging throughout this country today, and thank God, they are refusing to be silenced. Indeed, the Truth does stand out clear from error. All we have to do is take a closer look, bear witness, and then refuse to let anyone convince us that we're just hallucinating. Love, learning, and logic are no hallucinations. They stand out as clearly from error as water does from oil.

Glossary

Allah: God. This is simply the Arabic word for God, and as such it is not exclusive to Islam. Within the context of Islam, *Allah* refers to the same God of the Jewish and Christian traditions, and thus, Arabic speakers use the term *Allah* to refer to God in any and all other religious contexts, including Christianity and Judaism.

Fatwa: A legal edict issued by an alleged Islamic scholar and/or spiritual advisor. There is no discussion of these legal edicts anywhere within the Qur'an. The fatwa is a construct of individual authorities and the communities that choose to follow them. Countless fatwas are issued every day around the world, a great many of them simply in order to facilitate mundane legal or business transactions. If a given Muslim community chooses a particular Islamic scholar to lead the community, then that scholar may issue legal pronouncements (fatwas) binding only on the members of that community who chose him or her to lead.

Hadiths: The collection of sayings of the Prophet Muhammad, may peace and blessings be upon him, resulting from oral tradition and transmission, collected after his death. Unlike the Qur'an, the hadiths are not treated as revelation. Some hadiths are considered more verifiable, while others are considered more dubious.

Hajj: The pilgrimage to Mecca required of every Muslim who is physically and financially capable, at least once in his or her life.

Halal: Refers to permissible acts and consumables; such as halal meat, for example.

Haram: Refers to impermissible acts and consumables; such as pork and alcohol, for example.

Hijab: A human expression of modesty, particularly modest dress; such dress is the result of a personal interpretation and expression and varies considerably across cultures. Perhaps the most common expressions of outward *hijab* are head and body coverings for women, and beards, long sleeves, and pants for men.

Hijra:	Migration; specifically the Prophet Muhammad's migration from Mecca to Medina in 622 A.C.E.
Ijtihad:	Independent personal interpretation of the Qur'an and the Sunnah. *Ijtihad* is a very serious undertaking that requires a deep understanding of Islam. The following statements of the Prophet Muhammad reflect the great importance placed on learning in Islam, proper education being a prerequisite for *ijtihad:* "An hour's meditation on the work of the Creator is better than seventy years of prayer" (94); "Philosophy is the stray camel of the Faithful, take hold of it wherever ye come across it" (92); "Seek knowledge from the cradle to the grave" (93); "The acquisition of knowledge is a duty incumbent on every Muslim, male and female" (94); "The ink of the scholar is more holy than the blood of the martyr" (94).[1] Hence, not only is the acquisition of knowledge a requirement for every Muslim, but it also has the potential to bring one closer to God than even prayer, and as lessening the distance between oneself and God is the primary task of every Muslim who seeks divine guidance and companionship, learning is both essential to and inextricable from the full practice of Islam. Without that learning, moreover, a valid practice of *ijtihad* is impossible.
Iman:	Faith in One Omniscient, Benevolent, Merciful, and Compassionate God.
Islam:	Submission to God; derived from and resulting in peace.
Jihad:	Spiritual struggle, including both the internal struggle to achieve and maintain righteousness and the outward personal and collective struggle for justice.
Pillars:	The frequently cited five pillars of Islam are as follows:

1. Faith in one God (*iman*) and submission to that God (*islam*). This also includes belief in the Prophet Muhammad as His messenger, to whom the miracle of the Qur'an was revealed by the Angel Gabriel.

2. The practice of faith and submission through five daily prayers (*salat*).

3. The giving of charity to the poor, especially orphans and widows (*zakat*).

4. The fulfillment of self-purification through fasting during the holy month of Ramadan by all those who are healthy and able to do so.

5. The fulfillment of the pilgrimage to Mecca (Hajj) for every Muslim who is physically and financially capable, at least once in his or her life.

Qur'an: The Muslim holy book of revelation; Muslims consider the Qur'an the third and final divine revelation after the Old and New Testaments.

Ramadan: The holy month during which it is believed that the majority of the Qur'an was revealed to the Prophet Muhammad, may peace and blessings be upon him. Able Muslims fast from sunrise until sunset during this month, and this fast includes abstaining from food, water, sex, and the use of profane language between sunrise and sunset.

Salat: The five daily prayers; also referred to as *namaz* in Persian.

Shahada: Declaration of one's faith in Islam; the *shahada* consists of saying and believing the following words: "La ilaha il Allah, Muhammad-ur-Rasool-Allah" (There is only one God, and that is Allah [the God of the Abrahamic tradition], and Muhammad was his messenger).

Shari'ah: Islamic law based on the Sunnah and the Qur'an.

Sira: Relations of the actions of the Prophet Muhammad, may peace and blessings be upon him, resulting from oral tradition and transmission, collected after his death. Unlike the Qur'an, the *sira* are not treated as revelation. Some *sira* are considered more verifiable, while others are considered more dubious.

Sufism: Islamic mysticism, out of which many famous poets have emerged, such as Rumi, Hafiz, Jami, and Saadi.

Sunnah: The collected sayings (*hadiths*) and actions (*sira*) of the Prophet Muhammad.

Sunni/Shi'a: While there are indeed more distinct sects within Islam beyond simply Sunnis and Shi'ites, the notion of wide-ranging denominations within the faith is far less prevalent than it tends to be, for example, in Christianity. That being said, there is no denying the great emphasis that some people tend to place on the distinctions between Sunni and Shi'a Islam. Sunni Muslims constitute the great majority of all Muslims around the world (roughly 80–90 percent), while Shi'ites represent a significant minority of Muslims (living mostly in Iran, Lebanon, and Iraq).[2] This Sunni/Shi'a split began after the death of the Prophet Muhammad, despite the fact that the Qur'an explicitly renounces the creation of sects and divisions within Islam (30:31–32, 42:13–14, 43:64–65). At the source of the division between Sunni and Shi'a Islam lies the order and structure of the Caliphate, or religious and political leadership, directly following the death of the Prophet Muhammad. The Sunnis generally accept the first four caliphs chosen after the Prophet's death (Abu Bakr, Umar ibn al-Khattab, Uthman, and Ali) as legitimate and rightfully guided caliphs, while Shi'ites generally accept only the caliphate of Ali, considering the first three caliphs in fact to be usurpers.

Umma: The collective community of Muslims around the world.

Zakat: Required charitable donation for Muslims (at least 2.5 percent of one's income).

Notes

All of my citations to the Holy Qur'an are based on the translation of the text by Abdullah Yusuf Ali in *The Meaning of the Holy Qur'an* and are generally cited nearly verbatim. Yusuf Ali provides a translation of the Qur'an, along with voluminous and incredibly thorough footnotes, explanations, and summaries. Again, my citations herein are *nearly* verbatim from his translation—at times I have inserted my own understandings into the translations as well.

INTRODUCTION

1. Estimates vary widely. See http://www.census.gov/ipc/www/world.html and *The World Almanac and Book of Facts 2007*, 712. Although these statistics appear in the 2007 *World Almanac*, they represent data collected in mid-2004. Also see the Web site for the Pluralism Project (a Harvard research program on world religions sponsored by grants from the Ford Foundation, the Lilly Endowment Inc., the Pew Charitable Trusts, the North Star Fund, the Templeton Foundation, and the Milton Fund): http://www.pluralism.org/resources/ statistics/tradition.php#IslamI. The mission of the Pluralism Project is to "help Americans engage with the realities of religious diversity through research, outreach, and the active dissemination of resources." Also see Handwerk, "Islam Expanding Globally."

2. See Handwerk, "Islam Expanding Globally."

3. See the Pluralism Project: http://www.pluralism.org/resources/statistics/ tradition.php#IslamI.

4. See Howard Feinbert and Iain Murray, "How Many U.S. Muslims? Our Best Estimate," *Christian Science Monitor*, Nov. 29, 2001. Fienberg and Murray, analysts at the Statistical Assessment Service, a nonpartisan research organization, find that "while a precise figure remains elusive,"'2 million Muslims, give or take a few hundred thousand' appears to be America's most accurate number—for now." Also see "Muslim Population Inflated, Studies Find," *Los Angeles Times*, Oct. 25, 2001; "Studies Suggest Lower Count for Number of U.S. Muslims," *New York Times*, Oct. 25, 2001; "Number of U.S. Muslims Depends on Who's Counting," *Washington Post*, Oct. 24, 2001. All these articles are available at the Pluralism Project: http://www.pluralism.org/news/index.php?tags=2093#headline2093.

5. See the 2007 *World Almanac*, 712.

6. See http://www.pbs.org/itvs/caughtinthecrossfire/arab_americans.html.

CHAPTER 1   *Melody*

The epigraph is from a letter that Malcolm wrote to friends while he was on his pilgrimage (Hajj). See Haley and Malcolm X, *Autobiography of Malcolm X*, 366.

CHAPTER 2   *Roxana*

1. Figures are from the International Federation of Red Cross and Red Crescent Societies. For further details, see http://www.ifrc.org/what/disasters/response/iran.asp.

CHAPTER 3 *Matthew*

William Wirt, a nineteenth-century American attorney, was the ninth U.S. attorney general. After stepping down as the attorney general in 1831, Wirt defended the Cherokee people within the state of Georgia before the U.S. Supreme Court in *Cherokee Nation v. Georgia*. See Kennedy, *Memoirs of the Life of William Wirt*, 360.

CHAPTER 4: *Ameer*

The epigraph is widely attributed to Louis Armstrong, but I could not find a proper source or even the circumstances of the statement.

CHAPTER 5 *Sarah*

For the epigraph, please see Shapiro and Hentoff, *Hear Me Talkin' to Ya*, 201.
　　1. See http://www.alsarah.com for more information on Sarah's album, tour dates, lyrics, videos, etc.

CHAPTER 6 *Faisal R.*

"A Great Wagon" may be found in *Essential Rumi*, 36.

CHAPTER 7 *Sanida*

The epigraph may be found in Gold and Hessenmueller, *Best Thoughts of Best Thinkers*, 573.

CHAPTER 8 *Molham*

Galileo's letter is included in Drake, *Discoveries and Opinions of Galileo*. Galileo was brought before the Catholic Church's Holy Inquisition for endorsing the Copernican heliocentric model of the solar system, which claimed that the sun (not the earth) was at the center of the solar system. For this, he was held under house arrest for the last nine years of his life (1633–42). The Catholic Church, in 1983, through Pope John Paul II, accepted that Galileo might have been right. Nine years later, in 1992, the Church formally acknowledged that it had erred in condemning Galileo. See the Vatican's official Website: http://www.vatican.va/news.

CHAPTER 9 *Willow*

The song "On the Road to Find Out" may be found on the CD *Classics, Vol. 24*, A&M Records, 1990.
　　1. See http://www.theatlantic.com/doc/prem/200507/wilson, or Willow's Website: http://www.gwillowwilson.com.

CHAPTER 10   *Hafeeza*

The Mark Twain quote may be found in Evans et al., *And I Quote*, 334.

1. For further discussion of the distinctions and similarities between the Nation of Islam and traditional Islam, see Mustafa El-Amin's film *The Religion of Islam and the Nation of Islam: What Is the Difference?* For more information on the life of Malcolm X, see Haley and Malcolm X, *Autobiography of Malcolm X*. Also see Manning Marable's upcoming biography, tentatively titled *Malcolm X: A Life of Reinvention*.

CHAPTER 11   *Asra*

The epigraph is from "Proceedings: First Anniversary of the American Equal Rights Association Held at The Church of the Puritans, NY," May 9–10th, 1867." See Dance, *Honey, Hush!* 480.

1. Nomani, *Standing Alone in Mecca*, 7.
2. Nomani, *Standing Alone in Mecca*, 10.
3. Nomani, *Tantrika*, 2004.
4. Nomani, *Standing Alone in Mecca*, 21–22.
5. Nomani, *Standing Alone in Mecca*, 15.
6. Nomani, *Standing Alone in Mecca*, 20.
7. Nomani, *Standing Alone in Mecca*, 26.
8. Nomani, *Standing Alone in Mecca*, 70.

CHAPTER 12   *Faisal A.*

1. See http://www.msnbc.msn.com/id/13712248.
2. See http://www.cnn.com/2003/WORLD/europe/09/10/sept.11.ukposter.
3. See http://news.bbc.co.uk/2/hi/uk_news/4144792.stm.
4. See http://www.rainbownetwork.com/News/detail.asp?iData=17388&iCat=29&iChannel=2&nChannel=News&action=vote&poll=y&pData=795.
5. See http://www.safeyouth.org/scripts/faq/suicidefacts.asp.
6. See http://www.city-data.com/city/Ellington-Connecticut.html.

CONCLUSION

1. Ali, *Manual of Hadith*, 398.

GLOSSARY

1. For all these quotations, see Al-Suhrawardy, *Sayings of Mohammad*.
2. See the CIA World Factbook: https://www.cia.gov/cia/publications/factbook/index.html.

Cited, Consulted, and Suggested Readings

Abelard, Peter. *Dialogue of a Philosopher with a Jew and a Christian*. Trans. Pierre Aballard. Vol. 20. Toronto: The Pontifical Institute of Mediaeval Studies, 1979.

Ahmed, Leila. *Women and Gender in Islam: Historical Roots of a Modern Debate*. New Haven: Yale University Press, 1992.

Ali, Maulana Muhammad. *A Manual of Hadith*. 2nd ed. Lahore, Pakistan: Ahmadiyya Anjuman Ishaat Islam, 1990.

———. *The Muslim Prayer-Book*. Columbus, OH: Payette & Simms, 1939.

Al-Qur'an. Trans. Ahmed Ali. Princeton: Princeton University Press, 1984.

Al-Suhrawardy, Allama Sir Abdullah Al-Mamun, ed., trans., and coll. *The Sayings of Muhammad*. Secaucus, NJ: Citadel Press, 1999.

Armstrong, Karen. *Islam: A Short History*. New York: Modern Library, 2000.

———. *Muhammad: A Biography of the Prophet*. San Francisco: HarperSanFrancisco, 1993.

Aslan, Reza. *No god but God*. New York: Random House, 2005.

Dance, Daryl Cumber, ed. *Honey, Hush! An Anthology of African-American Women's Humor*. New York: W. W. Norton & Co., 1998.

Drake, Stillman, ed. and trans. *Discoveries and Opinions of Galileo*. New York: Doubleday Anchor Books, 1957.

El-Amin, Mustafa. *The Religion of Islam and the Nation of Islam: What Is the Difference?* Newark, NJ: El-Amin Productions, 1991.

Esack, Farid. *On Being Muslim: Finding a Religion's Path in the World Today*. Oxford: Oneworld Publications, 1999.

Esposito, John. *The Islamic Threat: Myth or Reality?* New York: Oxford University Press, 1992.

———, ed. *The Oxford History of Islam*. New York: Oxford University Press, 1999.

Evans, William R., Ashton Applewhite, Tripp Evans, and Andrew Frothingham. *And I Quote*. New York: St. Martin's Press, 2003.

Gold, Hialmer Day, and Edward Louis Hessenmueller. *Best Thoughts of Best Thinkers*. Cleveland: Best Thoughts Publishing Co., 1904.

Haddad, Yvonne Yazbeck, ed. *The Muslims of America*. New York: Oxford University Press, 1991.

Haley, Alex, and Malcolm X. *The Autobiography of Malcolm X*. 33rd ed. New York: Ballantine Books, 1992.

Handwerk, Brian. "Islam Expanding Globally, Adapting Locally." *National Geographic News*, October 24, 2003. http://news.nationalgeographic.com/news/2003/10/1022_031022_islamdiversity.html.

Hixon, Lex. *Heart of the Koran*. Wheaton, IL: The Theosophical Publishing House, 1988.

Jami. *Yusuf and Zulaikha*. Trans. David Pendlebury. London: Octagon Press, 1980.

Kennedy, John Pendleton. *Memoirs of the Life of William Wirt*. Philadelphia: Lea and Blanchard, 1849.

The Koran: Interpreted. Trans. A. J. Arberry. New York: Simon and Schuster, 1996.

Marable, Manning. *Malcolm X: A Life of Reinvention*. New York: Viking, forthcoming.

Mernissi, Fatima. *The Veil and the Male Elite: A Feminist Interpretation of Women's Rights in Islam*. Ed. Mary Jo Lakeland. Upper Saddle River, NJ: Addison-Wesley Publishing Co., 1992.

Nasr, Seyyed Hossein. *Ideals and Realities of Islam*. London: Harper Collins, 1966.

Nasr, Seyyed Hossein, and Oliver Leaman, eds. *History of Islamic Philosophy*. Vols. 1–2. Tehran: Arayeh, 1375 (1954 A.C.E.).

Nomani, Asra Q. *Standing Alone in Mecca*. San Francisco: HarperSanFrancisco, 2005.

———. *Tantrika*. San Francisco: HarperSanFrancisco, 2004.

Pape, Robert. *Dying to Win: The Strategic Logic of Suicide Terrorism*. New York: Random House, 2005.

Rumi. *The Essential Rumi*. Trans. Coleman Barks, with John Moyne, A. J. Arberry, and Reynold Nicholson. San Francisco: HarperSanFrancisco, 1995.

Shapiro, Nat, and Nat Hentoff, eds. *Hear Me Talkin' to Ya*. New York: Dover, 1955.

Shariati, Ali. *Hajj*. Trans. Ali Behzadnia and Najla Denny. Costa Mesa, CA: Jubilee Press, 1993.

Wadud, Amina. *Inside the Gender Jihad: Women's Reform in Islam*. New York: Oneworld, 2006.

———. *Qur'an and Woman: Rereading the Sacred Text from a Woman's Perspective*. New York: Oxford University Press, 1999.

Wilson, G. Willow. "Arguing in Mecca." *Parabola* 31 (Fall 2006): 62–66.

———. "The Show-Me Sheikh." *Atlantic Monthly*, July–August 2005. http://www.the atlantic.com/doc/prem/200507/wilson.

Wilson, G. Willow, and M. K. Perker. *Cairo*. New York: Vertigo, 2007.

The World Almanac and Book of Facts 2007. Ed. Zoe Kashner. New York: World Almanac Books, 2007.

X, Malcolm. *By Any Means Necessary*. New York: Pathfinder Press, 1992.

Yusuf Ali, Abdullah. *The Meaning of the Holy Qur'an*. Beltsville, MD: Amana Publications, 2001.

Zepp, Ira G. *A Muslim Primer: Beginner's Guide to Islam*. 2nd ed. Fayetteville: University of Arkansas Press, 1999.

Born in 1979, **Melody Moezzi** grew up mostly in Dayton, Ohio, amid a strong and vibrant Iranian American diaspora. She is an attorney, an activist, a freelance writer. Her work has appeared in *Dissident Voice, Urban Mozaik Magazine, American Chronicle, Parabola*, and the *Yale Journal for Humanities in Medicine*. Moezzi lives in Atlanta with her husband, Matthew, and their two cats, Olyan and Talula.

Abdullahi Ahmed An-Na'im is the Charles Howard Candler Professor of Law, Emory University School of Law, and the author of many books, including *African Constitutionalism and the Contingent Role of Islam; Toward an Islamic Reformation;* and *Human Rights, Religion and the Contingency of Universalist Projects*.